BEST
BLACK
SERMONS

Editor: William M. Philpot

Advisory Panel: Walter B. Hoard, Gardner
  C. Taylor, Colin W. Williams, Samuel W.
  Winslow

JUDSON PRESS ® VALLEY FORGE

To the membership of Christ Chapel New Testament Church, New Haven, Connecticut.

William M. Philpot

BEST BLACK SERMONS

Copyright © 1972
Judson Press, Valley Forge, PA 19482-0851

Note: This book was first published in 1972 and represents the language of that time.

Library of Congress Cataloging in Publication Data

Philpot, William M.   comp.
    Best Black Sermons.

    CONTENTS: Introduction, by G. C. Taylor.—Three dimensions of a complete life, by M. L. King, Jr.—Handicapped lives, by W. H. Borders, Sr. [etc.]
    1. Sermons, American—Negro authors. I. Title
BV4241.5.P48   252   72-75358
ISBN 0-8170-0533-1

Except where otherwise indicated, the Bible quotations in this volume are in accordance with the Revised Standard Version of the Bible, copyright © 1946 and 1952, by the Division of Christian Education of the National Council of the Churches of Christ in the United States of America, and are used by permission.

Printed in the U.S.A.
17 16 15 14 13 12 11
15 14 13 12 11 10 09 08 07 06 05 04 03 02 01 00 99 98 97 96

BEST
BLACK
SERMONS

CONTENTS

INTRODUCTION
Gardner C. Taylor

For a long time, the "joy-sorrow" quality of black music has been recognized as creative and classic. Strangely enough, only recently has the possibility been manifest that the black preacher, rising up out of heartbreak and hope, apostle at the same time of apocalyptic escape and determined protest, may have a "word of life" to speak to American society, now confused, frightened, insecure about its future, and uncertain about its basic assumptions.

This volume of sermons by an interesting and stimulating variety of black preachers will illustrate the vitality of the black church and the centrality of preaching which still characterize this principal institution of black America. In this volume will be found those "angles of vision" of the Scriptures and of human life not immediately and easily available to any preachers except those who are part of a disillusioned and disinherited community. Likewise, there will be seen here again and again a vivid imagery and a stubborn, strong, and splendid faith in that God who is more than match for men's evil structures of oppression and who supremely illustrated his power to overcome at Calvary. Through much of the preaching here one can almost detect the sound of a people, once slaves, who would not hang their harps in the willows when they sat down in a strange land by the waters of Babylon, but whose souls sang on, sometimes sadly and sometimes joyously, toward that deliverance and destiny which they have believed and still believe the Lord of their fathers has in store for them.

The following sermon by Martin Luther King, Jr., has been chosen for this book by the Advisory Panel because of Dr. King's outstanding reputation as a preacher in the black churches and as a national leader. Beginning with the bus boycott in Montgomery, Alabama, Martin Luther King, Jr., took a very active role in the drive for civil rights through nonviolent methods until his tragic assassination in Memphis, Tennessee, in 1968. Dr. King did his undergraduate work at Morehouse College and received his seminary education at Crozer Theological Seminary in Chester, Pennsylvania. He earned the Ph.D. degree at Boston University. Recipient of many awards, he received the Nobel Peace Prize in 1964.

THREE DIMENSIONS OF A COMPLETE LIFE
Martin Luther King, Jr.

"The length and the breadth and the height of it are equal" (Revelation 21:16). John the Revelator, imprisoned on a lonely, obscure island called Patmos, was deprived of almost every freedom except the freedom to think. So he thought about many things. He thought about the old political order and its tragic incompleteness and its horrible injustices. He thought about the old Jerusalem and its superficial piety and its perfunctory ritual-

From *Strength to Love* (New York: Harper & Row, Publishers, Inc., 1963), Copyright © 1963 by Martin Luther King, Jr. Reprinted by permission of Harper & Row, Publishers, Inc.

ism. But in the midst of his agonizing vision of the old, John also had a glorious vision of something new and great. He saw a new and holy Jerusalem descending out of heaven from God. The most noble thing about this new heavenly city was its completeness, radiant as daybreak ending the long night of stagnating incompleteness. It would not be partial or one-sided, but complete in all three of its dimensions. In describing the city, John says, "The length and the breadth and the height of it are equal." This new city of God would not be an unbalanced entity with towering virtues on one side and degrading vices on the other; it would be complete on all sides.

For many people the Book of Revelation is a strange book and puzzling to decode. It is often cast aside as an enigma wrapped in mystery. But beneath John's peculiar jargon and his prevailing apocalyptic symbolism, we find many challenging and profound truths. One such truth is set forth in our text. When John describes the new city of God, he is really describing ideal humanity. He is saying, in substance, that life at its best is complete on all sides.

In our individual and collective lives are a disturbing incompleteness and an agonizing partialness. Very seldom are we able to affirm greatness in an unqualified sense. Following almost every affirmation of greatness is the conjunction "but." Naaman "was a great man," says the Old Testament, "but—" That *but* reveals something tragic and disturbing. "But he was a leper." How much of man's life can be so described!

Greece was a great nation, which left for succeeding generations an inexhaustible treasury of knowledge. She gave to the world the poetic insights of Aeschylus, Sophocles, and Euripides, and the philosophical insights of Socrates, Plato, and Aristotle. Because of these great minds, each of us is an heir to a legacy of creative ideas. Greece was a great nation, but— That *but* underscores the tragic fact that Greece was really an aristocracy for *some* of the people and not a democracy for *all* of the people. That *but* stands for the ugly fact that the Greek city-states were built on a foundation of slavery.

Western civilization is a great civilization, bequeathing to the world the magnificent insights of the Renaissance; the glad thunders and the gentle sighings of Handel, the majestic sweetness of Beethoven, and the charming melodies of Bach; the industrial revolution and man's commencement on his marvelous trek toward the city of material abundance. Western civilization is great, but— That *but* reminds us of the injustices and evils of colonialism, and of a civilization that has permitted its material means to outdistance its spiritual ends.

America is a great nation, offering to the world, through the Declaration of Independence, the most eloquent and unequivocal expression of the dignity of man ever set forth in a sociopolitical document. In technology, America has produced mighty bridges to span the seas and skyscraping buildings to kiss the skies. Through the Wright brothers, she has given to the world the airplane and made it possible for man to annihilate distance and circumscribe time. Through medical science, her numerous wonder drugs have cured many dread diseases and greatly prolonged the life of man. America is a great nation, but— That *but* is a commentary on two hundred and more years of chattel slavery and on twenty million Negro men and women deprived of life, liberty, and the pursuit of happiness. That *but* stands for a practical materialism that is often more interested in things than values.

So almost every affirmation of greatness is followed, not by a period symbolizing completeness, but by a comma punctuating its nagging partialness. Many of our greatest civilizations are great only in certain aspects. Many of our greatest men are great only in certain ways and are low and degrading in other regards.

Yet life should be strong and complete on every side. Any complete life has the three dimensions suggested in our text— length, breadth, and height. The length of life is the inward drive to achieve one's personal ends and ambitions, an inward concern for one's own welfare and achievements. The breadth of life is the outward concern for the welfare of others. The height of life is the upward reach for God. Life at its best is a coherent triangle. At one angle is the individual person. At the other angle are other persons. At the tiptop is the Infinite Person, God. Without the due development of each part of the triangle, no life can be complete.

I

Let us turn, first, to the length of life or the individual's concern about developing his inner powers. In a sense this is the selfish dimension of life. There is such a thing as rational and healthy self-interest. The late Rabbi Joshua Liebman pointed out in an interesting chapter in his book *Peace of Mind* that we must love ourselves properly before we can adequately love others. Many people are plunged into the abyss of emotional fatalism because they do not love themselves in a wholesome way.

Every person must have a concern for self and feel a responsibility to discover his mission in life. God has given each normal person a capacity to achieve some end. True, some are endowed with more talent than others, but God has left none of us talentless. Potential powers of creativity are within us, and we have the duty to work assiduously to discover these powers.

After one has discovered what he is made for, he should surrender all of the power in his being to the achievement of this. He should seek to do it so well that nobody could do it better. He should do it as though God Almighty called him at this particular moment of history for this reason. No one ever makes a great contribution to humanity without this majestic sense of purpose and this dogged determination. No one ever brings his potentiality into actuality without this powerful inner drive. Longfellow wrote:

> The heights by great men reached and kept
> Were not attained by sudden flight,
> But they, while their companions slept,
> Were toiling upward in the night.

May I offer a special word to our young people. The dimension of length stands as a unique challenge. Many of you are in college and many more in high school. I cannot overemphasize the importance of these years of study. You must realize that doors of opportunity are opening now that were not opened to your mothers and fathers. The great challenge you face is to be ready to enter these doors. You must early discover what you are made for, and you must work indefatigably to achieve excellence in your various fields of endeavor. Ralph Waldo Emerson has been quoted as saying, "If a man can write a better book, preach a better sermon, or make a better mousetrap than his neighbour, tho' he build his house in the woods, the world will make a beaten path to his door." This will become increasingly true. You must not wait until the day of full emancipation before you make a creative contribution to the life of this nation. Although you experience a natural dilemma as a result of the legacy of slavery and segregation, inferior schools, and second-class citizenship, you must with determination break through the outer shackles of circumstance. We already have inspiring examples of Negroes who in cloudfilled nights of oppression have become new and blazing stars of achievement. From an old slave cabin in Virginia's hills, Booker T. Washington rose to become one of America's great leaders. From the oppressive red hills of Gordon County, Georgia, and the arms of a mother who could neither read nor write, Roland Hayes emerged as one of the world's foremost singers, whose melodious voice was heard in the palaces of kings and the mansions of queens. Coming from a poverty-stricken environment in Philadelphia, Marian Anderson achieved the distinction of being the world's greatest contralto, and so much so that Toscanini said that a voice like hers comes only once in a century and Sibelius exclaimed that his roof was too low for such a voice. From crippling circumstance, George Washington Carver made for himself an imperishable niche in the annals of science. Ralph J. Bunche, the grandson of a slave preacher, has brought a rare distinction to diplomacy. These are only a few of the numerous examples which remind us that, in spite of our lack of full freedom, we can make a contribution here and now.

We are challenged on every hand to work untiringly to achieve excellence in our lifework. Not all men are called to specialized or professional jobs; even fewer rise to the heights of genius in the arts and sciences; many are called to be laborers in factories, fields, and streets. But no work is insignificant. All labor that uplifts humanity has dignity and importance and should be undertaken with painstaking excellence. If a man is called to be a street sweeper, he should sweep streets even as Michelangelo painted, or Beethoven composed music, or Shakespeare wrote poetry. He should sweep streets so well that all the host of heaven and earth will pause to say, "Here lived a great street sweeper who did his job well." This is what Douglas Mallock meant when he wrote:

> If you can't be a pine on the top of the hill
> Be a scrub in the valley—but be
> The best little scrub by the side of the rill,
> Be a bush, if you can't be a tree.

> If you can't be a highway, just be a trail
> If you can't be the sun, be a star;
> It isn't by size, that you win or fail—
> Be the best of whatever you are.

Set yourself earnestly to discover what you are made to do, and then give yourself passionately to the doing of it. This clear onward drive toward self-fulfillment is the length of a man's life.

II

Some people never get beyond this first dimension. They may be brilliant people who superbly develop their inner powers, but they are shackled by the chains of a paralyzing self-centeredness. They live within the narrow confines of their personal ambitions and desires. What is more tragic than to find an individual who is bogged down in the length of life devoid of breadth?

If life is to be complete, it must include not only the dimension of length but also of breadth by which the individual concerns himself in the welfare of others. No man has learned to live until he can rise above the narrow confines of his individualistic concerns to the broader concerns of all humanity. Length without breadth is like a self-contained tributary having no outward flow to the ocean. Stagnant, still, and stale, it lacks both life and freshness. In order to live creatively and meaningfully, our self-concern must be wedded to other-concern.

When Jesus painted that symbolic picture of the great assize, he made it clear that the norm for determining the division between the sheep and the goats would be deeds done for others. One will not be asked how many academic degrees he obtained or how much money he acquired, but how much he did for others. Did you feed the hungry? Did you give a cup of cold water to the thirsty? Did you clothe the naked? Did you visit the sick and minister to the imprisoned? These are the questions asked by the Lord of life. In a sense every day is judgment day, and we, through our deeds and words, our silence and speech, are constantly writing in the Book of Life.

Light has come into the world, and every man must decide whether he will walk in the light of creative altruism or the darkness of destructive selfishness. This is the judgment. Life's most persistent and urgent question is, "What are you doing for others?"

God has so structured this universe that things do not quite work out rightly if men are not diligent in their cultivation of the dimension of breadth. "I" cannot reach fulfillment without "thou." The self cannot be self without other selves. Social psychologists tell us that we cannot truly be persons unless we interact with other persons. All life is interrelated, and all men are interdependent. And yet we continue to travel a road paved with the slippery cement of inordinate selfishness. Most of the tragic problems we are confronting in the world today mirror man's failure to add breadth to length.

This is clearly seen in the racial crisis facing our nation. The tension in race relations is a result of the fact that many of our white brothers are inordinately concerned in the length of life—their economically privileged positions, their political power, their social status, their so-called "way of life." If only they would add breadth to length—the other-regarding dimension to the self-regarding dimension—the jangling discords in our nation would be transformed into a beautiful symphony of brotherhood.

This need for adding breadth to length is also to be seen in international relations. No nation can live alone. Mrs. King and I were privileged to make a memorable visit to India. Although there were many high and rewarding moments, there were also many depressing moments during our journey through India. How can one avoid being depressed when he sees with his own eyes millions of people who go to bed hungry? How can one avoid being depressed when he sees with his own eyes millions of people sleeping on the sidewalk? How can one avoid being depressed when he learns that 350,000,000 of India's population of more than 435,000,000 people make an annual income of less than $70 per year, and is told that most of them have never seen a doctor or a dentist?

Can we in America remain unconcerned about these conditions? The answer is emphatically no. Our destiny as a nation is linked to the destiny of India. So long as India, or any other nation, is insecure, we shall never be secure. We must use our vast resources of wealth to aid the undeveloped countries of the world. Have we spent far too much of our national budget in establishing military bases around the world and far too little in establishing bases of genuine concern and understanding?

In the final analysis, all men are interdependent and are thereby involved in a single process. We are inevitably our brother's keeper because of the interrelated structure of reality. No nation or individual can live in isolation. John Donne interpreted this truth in graphic terms when he affirmed:

> No man is an Iland, intire of its selfe; every man is a peece of the Continent, a part of the maine; if a Clod bee washed away by the Sea, Europe is the lesse, as well as if a Promontorie were, as well as if a Mannor of thy friends or of thine owne were; any mans death diminishes me, because I am involved in Mankinde; And therefore never send to know for whom the bell tolls; It tolls for thee.

This recognition of the oneness of humanity and the need of an active brotherly concern for the welfare of others is the breadth of man's life.

III

One more dimension of the complete life remains, namely, the height or that upward reach toward something distinctly greater than humanity. We must rise above earth and give our ultimate allegiance to that eternal Being who is the source and ground of all reality. When we add height to length and breadth, we have the complete life.

Just as there are some people who never get beyond length, so there are others who never get beyond the combination of length and breadth. They brilliantly develop their inner powers, and they have a genuine humanitarian concern. But they stop short. They are so earth-bound that they conclude that humanity is God. They seek to live without a sky.

There are probably several reasons why modern man has neglected this third dimension. Some men have honest intellectual doubts. Looking upon the horrors of moral and natural evil, they ask, "If there is a good God who is all-powerful, why does he permit such unmerited pain and suffering to exist?" Their inability adequately to answer this question leads them into agnosticism. And there are those who also find it difficult to square their scientific and rationalistic findings with the sometimes unscientific dogmas of religion and the primitive conceptions of God.

I suspect, however, that a majority of people fit into still another category. They are not theoretical atheists; they are practical atheists. They do not deny the existence of God with their lips, but they are continually denying his existence with their lives. They live as though there is no God. This erasing of God from the agenda of life may well have been an unconscious process. Most men do not say, "Good-by God, I am going to leave you now." But they become so involved in the things of this world that they are unconsciously carried away by the rushing tide of materialism and are left treading in the confused waters of secularism. Modern man, living in what Professor Sorokin has called "a sensate culture," believes only those things which can be known by the five senses.

But this attempt to substitute a man-centered universe for a God-centered universe leads only to deeper frustration. Reinhold Niebuhr has said, "Since 1914 one tragic event has followed another as if history were designed to refute the vain delusions of modern man." We sail upon the seas of modern history like a ship without a compass. We have neither a guide nor a sense of direction. We doubt our doubts, and wonder whether, after all, there may not in truth be some spiritual force undergirding reality.

In spite of our theoretical denials, we have spiritual experiences that cannot be explained in materialistic terms. In spite of our worship of the natural order, ever and again we feel impinging upon us something that causes us to wonder how the magnificent orderliness of the universe can be the result of a fortuitous interplay of atoms and electrons. In spite of our inordinate reverence for material things, ever and again something reminds us of the reality of the unseen. At night we look up at the stars which bedeck the heavens like swinging lanterns of eternity. For the moment we may think we see all, but something reminds us that we do not see the law of gravitation that holds them there. Enraptured, we gaze at the architectural beauty of some impressive house of God, but soon something reminds us that our eyes cannot behold that cathedral in its total reality. We have not seen within the mind of the architect who drew the blueprint. We can never see the love and the faith of the individuals whose sacrifices made the construction possible. Looking at each other, we quickly conclude that our perception of the physical body is a vision of all that we are. As you presently gaze at the pulpit and witness me preaching this sermon, you may immediately conclude that you see Martin Luther King. But then you are reminded that you see only my body, which in itself can neither reason nor think.

You can never see the *me* that makes me me, and I can never see the *you* that makes you you. That invisible something we call personality is beyond our physical gaze. Plato was right when he said that the visible is a shadow cast by the invisible.

God is still in his universe. Our new technological and scientific developments can neither banish him from the microcosmic compass of the atom nor from the vast, unfathomable ranges of interstellar space. Living in a universe in which the distances of some heavenly bodies must be dated in terms of billions of light years, modern man exclaims with the Psalmist of old, "When I consider thy heavens, the work of thy fingers, the moon and the stars, which thou hast ordained; what is man, that thou art mindful of him? and the son of man, that thou visitest him?"

I would urge you to give priority to search for God. Allow his spirit to permeate your being. To meet the difficulties and challenges of life you will need him. Before the ship of your life reaches its last harbor, there will be long, drawn-out storms, howling and jostling winds, and tempestuous seas that make the heart stand still. If you do not have a deep and patient faith in God, you will be powerless to face the delays, disappointments, and vicissitudes that inevitably come. Without God, all of our efforts turn to ashes and our sunrises into darkest nights. Without him, life is a meaningless drama in which the decisive scenes are missing. But with him, we are able to rise from tension-packed valleys to the sublime heights of inner peace, and find radiant stars of hope against the nocturnal bosom of life's most depressing nights. St. Augustine was right: "Thou hast created us for thyself, and our heart cannot be quieted till it find repose in thee."

A wise old preacher went to a college to deliver a baccalaureate sermon. After finishing his message, he lingered on the campus to talk with members of the graduating class. He spoke with a brilliant young graduate named Robert. His first question to Robert was: "What are your plans for the future?" "I plan to go immediately to law school," said Robert. "What then, Robert?" inquired the preacher. "Well," responded Robert, "I plan to get married and start a family and then get myself securely established in my law practice." "What then, Robert?" continued the preacher. Robert retorted, "I must frankly say that I plan to make lots of money from my law practice and thereby I hope to retire rather early and spend a great deal of time traveling to various parts of the world—something that I have always wanted to do." "What then, Robert?" added the preacher with an almost annoying inquisitiveness. "Well," said Robert, "these are all of my plans." Looking at Robert with a countenance expressing pity and fatherly concern, the preacher said, "Young man, your plans are far too small. They can extend only seventy-five or a hundred years at the most. You must make your plans big enough to include God and large enough to include eternity."

This is wise advice. I suspect that all too many of us are still dabbling with plans that are big in quantity, but small in quality, plans that move on the horizontal plane of time rather than on the vertical plane of eternity. I, too, would urge you to make your plans so large and broad that they cannot be bound by the chains of time and the manacles of space. Give your life—all you have and are—to the God of the universe whose purpose changeth not.

Where do we find this God? In a test tube? No. Where else except in Jesus Christ, the Lord of our lives? By knowing him we know God. Christ is not only Godlike but God is Christlike. Christ is the word made flesh. He is the language of eternity translated in the words of time. If we are to know what God is like and understand his purposes for mankind, we must turn to Christ. By committing ourselves absolutely to Christ and his way, we will participate in that marvelous act of faith that will bring us to the true knowledge of God.

What then is the conclusion of the matter? Love yourself, if that means rational and healthy self-interest. You are commanded to do that. That is the length of life. Love your neighbor as you love yourself. You are commanded to do that. That is the breadth of life. But never forget that there is a first and even greater commandment: "Love the Lord thy God with all thy heart, and with all thy soul, and with all thy mind." This is the height of life. Only by a painstaking development of all three of these dimensions can you expect to live a complete life.

Thank God for John who, many centuries ago, lifted his vision to high heaven and there saw the new Jerusalem in all of its magnificence. God grant that we, too, will catch the vision and move with unrelenting passion toward that city of complete life in which the length and the breadth and the height are equal. Only by reaching this city can we achieve our true essence. Only by attaining this completeness can we be true sons of God.

William Holmes Borders, Sr., is pastor of the Wheat Street Baptist Church in Atlanta, Georgia. He came to this church from the pastorate of Second Baptist Church in Evanston, Illinois. A native of Georgia, he earned the Bachelor of Arts degree from Morehouse College in Atlanta, as an honor student, even though he entered under probation because he did not have a full high school education. He went on to earn the Bachelor Divinity degree from Garrett Theological Seminary, and the Master of Arts degree from Northwestern University. He has received honorary doctorates from many colleges and universities. Dr. Borders has been active in civic affairs in Atlanta and has written several books. He is a board member for many organizations, including the Board of Trustees of Morris Brown College.

HANDICAPPED LIVES
William Holmes Borders, Sr.

The other day at Tuskegee Institute I visited the cemetery. I came to a tombstone. It read: "GEORGE WASHINGTON CARVER—Died in Tuskegee, Alabama, January 5, 1943. A Life that stood out as a gospel of Self-Forgetful Service. He could have added Fortune to Fame, but caring for neither, he found happiness and honour in being helpful to the world."

The center of his world was the South where he was born in slavery some years ago, and in the South he did his work as a creative scientist.

I reread the inscription as I removed my hat. I said to myself,

"Not only was Carver a creative scientist but a blessed saint." I thought of his sickly body. I thought of how he was expected to die. I thought of how he was stolen and later swapped for a horse. I thought of how he made a garage laundry more popular than the college president's office. I thought of how he earned a master's degree at Iowa. I thought of Booker T. Washington bringing him to Tuskegee. I thought of the first time I met Carver. He wore greasy, ragged clothes. I thought of how he painted beautiful pictures with the ends of his fingers. I thought of how with those same fingers he played a piano. I thought of how he surmounted every obstacle in his path, climbing higher and higher until his recognition reached international proportions. I said to myself as I left that cemetery, "A handicap can be a blessing."

My host whizzed me to the art department of the Institute. One of the students asked that I describe the aid that "art" could be to religion. At the close, I was told of an artist who had been sick for twenty-five years. I insisted that I be taken to his home. His wife was energetic, immaculate, and orderly. He had been flat on his back a quarter of a century, unable even to brush his teeth. The secret of his personality was revealed in his eyes. They sparkled more brilliantly than stars. He told his story. He reads all day. He has an improvised rack. The book is clinched with clothespins, so are the pages. His wife turns the pages and pins them for him. He reads while she does other things in the house. His granddaughter is his secretary. His body is dead. He writes poetry with his head. I came out of that home thanking God for its consecration and devotion. "A handicap can be a blessing."

My mind raced from Tuskegee to Atlanta. I remembered Charles Moseley in his blindness. His wife and three daughters rallied around his infirmity. The ends of his fingers developed eyes. He saw through blinded eyes how to build a house. Neighbors once called the police to make him come down off the roof where he had climbed to repair a leak. In my mind I pitied him once. Then it dawned on me that he had a pocketbook full of money, that he repaired his house, that he collected his rent, that he was independent, that he supported his family, that he had done better blind than I had with eyes. Yes, it dawned on me that he did not need any pity. His blindness was the source of his power. Through his weakness God had made him strong.

My mind moved from Moseley to a blind paper boy on the west side. I came across him one Sunday morning when I was late for my broadcast. He was on Hunter Street. I pulled up in my car and called, "Heh, here!" He stopped. This paper boy wore white slacks and a flopped hat. He said, "Who is this who knows me?"

I said, "This is Reverend Borders."

"Yes, I hear you all the time. I know you!" he replied.

I asked, "How long have you been carrying papers?"

"Nearly twenty-three years," he answered.

"What's your name?"

"Kelley."

"How do you know where these houses are?" I asked.

"I know how many steps I take. I can tell the feel of the pavement."

"How do you know when to cross the street?"

"I can see with my ears."

"Are you married?"

"I've been married."

"Have you got any children?"

"One boy, five years old—that is, he was five when my wife got her divorce."

"So your wife got a divorce?"

"Yes, and took all I had."

"How much did you have?"

"About $2000. I oughta give her another thousand!"

"For what?"

"It was worth an extra thousand to get rid of her," he concluded. I pulled away saying, "I'll see you."

"All right, Reverend Borders."

My cup was already full—this ran it over.

Everybody has an infirmity. Everybody has a weakness. Everybody has a defect. Everybody has a disease. Everybody has a problem. Everybody has an obstacle. Everybody has a difficulty. It may be cancer. It may be mental frustration. It may be spiritual inequity. It may be an unbalanced complex. Maybe you want to curse the moral order because you are Negro. Loneliness may be knocking at your door. Old age may be creeping up on you. Whatever it is, face it as a fact. Work within that limitation. That limitation is where your strength ends. It is where God's power begins. God says, "You are the creature. I am the Creator. You are finite. I am infinite. You have power. I have all power." In your weakness you are made strong. The limitation caused by your weakness is God's chance to prove his power.

The uncured disease of a woman gave God's power through Jesus a chance. Lazarus's death was Jesus' opportunity to prove himself master over the grave. The cross gave Jesus the best chance he had to pray. Joseph's tomb gave Jesus his best chance to conquer the world with all human odds against him.

One day I stopped by the home of Paul Laurence Dunbar; he gave one verse:

> A crust of bread and a corner to sleep in,
> A minute to smile and an hour to weep in,
> A pint of joy to a peck of trouble,
> And never a laugh but the moans come double:
> And that is life! [1]

I remembered that he was tubercular and was dead before he was thirty-five.

Another day I opened my Bible to the Book of Daniel. In spirit I was dragged from Jerusalem to the Babylonian captivity. Slavery had cut the hearts of some Jews into a thousand pieces. Babylonian slave music was brought up-to-date in Psalm 137:

> "By the rivers of Babylon we sat down. Yea, we wept when we remembered Zion."
> We yearned for home. We wanted fellowship and union with our sisters and brothers. The empty loneliness of Babylon brought sorrow to our hearts and tears to our eyes.
> "There they that carried us away captive required of us song. And they that wasted us required of us mirth, saying, 'Sing us one of the songs of Zion.' "

"How can we sing the Lord's song in a strange land?" (See Psalm 137:1, 3, 4). How can slaves shout for joy? How can we be happy chained in slavery? How can the clink of iron chains be converted into musical harmony? How can your heart sing when your body sags under fetters of iron? How can a mocking bird sing with a broken wing? How can a rabbit run with a broken leg? How can we sing—miles from home with a dagger in our hearts? Some do best under a handicap.

[1] Paul Laurence Dunbar, *The Complete Poems of Paul Laurence Dunbar* (New York: Dodd, Mead & Co., 1970), pp. 9-10.

Bermuda grass grows best when you try to kill it. A certain kind of apple tree, gashed, yields its best fruit. Negro spirituals were born in dark days of bondage when trials were hard. Beethoven, who was deaf, composed eternal harmonies for other people's ears. A pearl is the result of disease in an oyster. John Milton peeped into paradise through blinded eyes. Moses was on his way when he chose "rather to suffer affliction with the people of God, than to enjoy the pleasures of sin for a season" (Hebrews 11:25, KJV). As the blaze leaped about her body, singeing her hair, Joan of Arc declared, "I have heard the voice of God; His voice must be obeyed."

Shadrach, Meshach, and Abednego, dumped into the fire by Nebuchadnezzar, refused to bow. Adversity carried Job's casket to his bedside—obnoxious, diseased, bankrupt, wounded by death, discouraged by his wife, forsaken and forgotten by friends, this ancient saint's heart forced his lips to utter, "When he hath tried me, I shall come forth as gold" (Job 23:10, KJV). On land, Paul's best prayer was in jail. On sea, Paul's best prayer was in a storm. Deacon Stephen's best prayer was in a ditch with stones bouncing off his skull. Jesus prayed best with his hands and feet spiked to a cross. Banished on the Isle of Patmos, John said, "I was in the Spirit on the Lord's day . . ." (Revelation 1:10, KJV). David was at his best, not sitting on a throne, wearing robes of purple and gold, but rather in the Twenty-third Psalm, passing through the valley and shadow of death. He cried out, "I will fear no evil: for thou art with me; thy rod and thy staff they comfort me. Thou preparest a table before me in the presence of mine enemies" (Psalm 23:4-5, KJV). When Herod severed John the Baptist's head from his body, that dead head rolled and preached God's word with greater power.

Suffering in Babylon, the Jew bounced back: "If I forget thee, O Jerusalem, let my right hand forget her cunning . . . let my tongue cleave to the roof of my mouth; if I prefer not Jerusalem above my chief joy" (Psalm 137:5-6, KJV). Let me remember that God can give me *joy in sorrow, victory in defeat, light in darkness,* and *success in failure.*

Paul declared to the Corinthians: "I glory in my infirmity. I have a thorn in the flesh." It pricked deep. It twisted around in the muscle. It pained. It ached. It irked. It hurt until my whole body was a ceaseless wave of torture. My mind could not function. My soul was wounded by this thorn reaching through the flesh. My existence was impaired. This thorn in the flesh reduced me to a couch. I tossed and tumbled. I tried remedy after remedy without relief. This thorn in the flesh handled me roughly. It was gnawing my life away. It baffled medical skill. It had my body. It was disturbing my mind. It was mixing poison for my spirit. (See 2 Corinthians 12.)

Curable disease is bad enough. Incurable disease is a torture. Physically curable diseases are handled by doctors. Incurables are handled by God. "Earth has no sorrow that heaven cannot heal." Somebody here now is an incurable. God has an absolute prescription. When the spirit strikes fire, it will be a signal that the perfect universal Doctor is waiting and willing to cure all diseases. Sick women! Diseased men! Take your case to God.

Paul did it. Diseased, pained, uncured, baffled—Paul sought the Lord. Said he: "I sought the Lord once." No answer came. "I sought the Lord twice. My weakness remained. I sought the Lord thrice."

I imagine Paul spread himself before God saying, "I am your servant; you are my God. I am tortured and pained without end. I have done all I know. I have preached 'prayer.' I have preached 'power.' I have preached 'ability.' Now I am caught with a thorn in the flesh which I can't master. I prayed once. I prayed twice. This is a third time. I need a personal answer. When it stormed, you sent an angel. When I was in Philippi, you rocked the jail. When I was trapped, you let me down over the Macedonian wall. When I was headed for Damascus to raise hell, you blocked the traffic. When I was stoned, you saved me. I need a personal answer to my plea. You made my body. A master mechanic knows his product. I have the faith in God, and you have the power."

Paul expected God to come by land, and he came by sea. God does not always answer prayer the way we want, or expect, but rather his way. God answered Elijah with a raven. God answered Moses with manna from on high. God answered Jesus by increasing a fish sandwich to a supermarket in the wilderness. God answered Joshua at Jericho with tumbling walls. God answered our slave parents with Sherman's march from Atlanta to the sea. God answered Gideon with three hundred who lapped water. God answered Elijah by fire. God answered Isaiah with fire. God answered Noah in the flood with an ark. God answered Paul on a stormy sea with an angel. God answered Jesus on the stormy sea of Galilee with personal power when Jesus said, "Peace be still." God answered Stephen in a ditch being stoned to death. God answered Gandhi enabling him to give the Hindu salute of forgiveness as bullets of death killed his body. God answered Jesus as murderers ripped his body. God answers not always the way you want or expect. Paul declares that after a third prayer God told him, "My grace is sufficient . . ." (2 Corinthians 12:9, KJV).

Paul moved on to write fourteen of the twenty-seven books in the New Testament. Scholars differ. Proof and disproof multiply Paul's greatness. He produced perhaps the greatest ode on love. He wrote a treatise on faith. His three major missionary journeys qualify him as one of the greatest. His prayers are religiously disturbing. His organizing of churches is gripping. His use of time behind iron bars writing solutions to church problems upset magistrates. His fiery gospel upset rulers. His easy use of several languages made him ready. In spite of handicaps of flesh, travel, jails, and persecution, Paul was second only to Jesus.

Dr. D. E. King is the minister of the Monumental Baptist Church in Chicago, Illinois. He has previously been pastor of the Friendship Baptist Church of New York City and churches in Kentucky, including Zion Baptist Church in Louisville. A native of Tennessee, he received the A.B. degree from LeMoyne College in Memphis, the M.A. and B.D. degrees from Howard University, and he received the D.D. degree from Simmons University. Dr. King is a charter member of the board of operation PUSH (People United to Save Humanity), a life member of the N.A.A.C.P., Chairman, Trustee Board, Nannie Helen Burroughs School, and a board member of the American Baptist Home Mission Societies, in addition to many other responsibilities.

THE GOD WHO TAKES OFF CHARIOT WHEELS
D. E. King

By right of our divine creation, all people everywhere have an insatiable desire to have an adequate share in humanity and in the commonwealth of creation. This is true of all persons, black, white, brown, red, "polka dot," or whatever the abortive identification.

From the very beginning, God established the law of liberation in the moral nature of the universe. Likewise, he also stamped his indestructible spirit of freedom into the very structure of human personality. These two divinely creative powers, the law of liberation in nature and the ineradicable spirit of freedom in human personality, combine to be "delivered from the bondage of corruption into the glorious liberty of the children of God." For this reason, "the whole creation groaneth and travaileth in pain together until now" (Romans 8:21-22, KJV). This law of liberation and this spirit of freedom are of such heavenly concern that no ruler, power structure, system, or government can outlaw or overrule them. Any attempt to suspend, abridge, or obstruct these basic inherent rights of liberation causes divine intervention. Before God allows any defiance against his ongoing purpose of love and freedom, he will wreck any power or system.

That is what happened to Egypt. For 430 years, her human wheels of slave labor zoomed. When the unpaid and unappreciated Hebrews had accelerated the wheels of Egyptian industry to the breaking point of no return, according to the text in Exodus 14:24-25, God intervened: "And it came to pass, that in the morning watch the Lord looked unto the Egyptians . . . and took off their chariot wheels." In the light of Egypt's prancing horses and speeding chariots, we should take a look at ourselves, our nation, and our world.

I

Let us begin with the divine purpose of all governments. From the beginning of time the wheels of history have moved toward the development and liberation of peoples through various forms of governments imposed from without. There are endless accounts of primitive peoples who have evolved into tribes, races, cities, fatherlands, dynasties, nations, and every conceivable form of government. They have been ruthlessly used against their own thrust toward freedom. Wars have been fought for power, for building empires, for enslaving minorities, for oppressing the masses, and for countless other excuses. But back of the idea of all governments is the universal consciousness of the oneness of the human spirit, moving toward the divine goal of human development and liberation. For that reason, the oppressed have operated the wheels of national and international governments for the purpose of bringing all the peoples of the earth into liberation and security.

Therefore, those who are in positions as leaders or rulers of any form of government have been entrusted with divine responsibilities of releasing the captives and of declaring the acceptable year of the Lord. This is what the apostle Paul had in mind when he counseled the Roman Christians: "Let every soul be subject unto the higher powers. For there is no power but of God. . . . For rulers are not a terror to good works, but to the evil" (Romans 13:1, 3, KJV).

This admonition applies to any government, whether it calls itself a dictatorship, a democracy, or communism. The officers and offices of such governments are ordained of God for the purpose of providing an equitable quality of life for the full development of all peoples, according to their maximum potentialities and possibilities. When this divinely ordained purpose is violated, God intervenes and impedes and sometimes wrecks all wheels and plans that are moving in the opposite direction of his ultimate destiny of justice and freedom for all. Egypt is an ancient example. God took off that nation's chariot wheels that were speeding against the march of the Hebrew slaves toward freedom. Germany is a contemporary exhibit. America, Russia, South Africa, and lesser nations are also on the agenda to be wrecked unless they change the course of their speeding wheels that lead to "the destruction that wasteth at noonday" (Psalm 91:6, KJV). When governmental officials create, promote, and maintain inequitable and iniquitous systems, God steps in and wrecks the entire operation on behalf of the weak and the helpless.

II

Now see how a misuse of powers, ordained of God, leads to self-idolatry. History is replete with instances when rulers or systems have assumed the power of deity. These instances are traceable from Egyptian bondage to Russian communism and to American imperialism. When such self-imposed powers vaunt themselves against the people of God, they become an affront to Jehovah himself. Therefore, they have to be dealt with.

Today the leaders of Russia and of America should learn a lesson from Pharaoh Rameses II. These two powers are mentioned because they claim to be the most powerful nations in the world today. Such claims have been held before by Babylon, Greece, Rome, England, and Germany under Hitler. There was a time when Britains boasted that the sun never set on British soil. Now England has been reduced to the extent that the sun sets on it anywhere. By the same token, the wheels of industry have sped Russia and America into dominant world positions. Russia does not conceal her imposed materialistic deity. America is equally as guilty, but she has, at least, erected a chapel in the White House to give religious sanction to her idolatrous power structure.

That is the reason why people of all races, cultures, and persuasions are rising up in rebellion against the power structure in America. There is an inborn alarm system in the spirit of man that turns on when rulers of governments assume self-idolatry.

It is amazing that leaders of American national, state, and local governments do not seem to see the handwriting on the wall. Like Egypt, we are at the height of prosperity. Our human and natural resources cannot be matched anywhere in the whole world. But we have deified these material resources. We are defying all world powers with our scientific advance and military strength plus our strategic bases around the world. This monopoly of self-idolatrous power has imposed itself in the very center of our national life, thus assigning God to the periphery.

In Egypt there were gods whom the Egyptians worshiped. The Pharaohs recognized these gods. But when the population explosion of the Hebrews got out of hand, Pharaoh Rameses II presumed the powers of the gods. He set himself up as the self-ordained ruling power, subject to no power outside of himself. But there was an Almighty Power with which Rameses had to deal; and in Pharaoh's wheeling and dealing, he was wrecked in the process. Self-imposed deification is as deceiving as a rooster which thinks that day breaks because he crows.

As God, the Almighty, looked unto the Egyptians, he is also looking unto the hosts of the Russians and of the Americans, and unto any other nation that deifies itself in defiance of God's ultimate purpose of liberation. His unalterable command is: "Thou shalt have no other gods before me."

III

Finally, see what happens when rulers of nations pigeonhole all options at their disposal to liberate people. Before Moses came on the scene, the struggle of Hebrew slaves spanned a period of 430 years. At that time no one dared to stand up against the unchallenged tyranny of Egypt. God needed a man with steeled courage and outraged indignation against the galling yoke of bondage. The late Dr. Vernon Johns said that "God discovered that man when Moses killed the Egyptian for brutally beating a helpless and defenseless Hebrew slave. It was then that God summoned an angel to 'go down and get that man's name and address; for I can use him.' "

Later Moses received the call of God without even being reprimanded for giving the Egyptian an immediate burial in self-defense. God commanded Moses to go and tell Pharaoh to "Let my people go." To this command, Pharaoh retorted: "Who is the Lord, that I should obey his voice to let Israel go? I know not the Lord, neither will I let Israel go" (Exodus 5:1-2, KJV).

From then on Moses was left to negotiate with Pharaoh until all options had been exhausted. You see, God's purpose for human freedom is too big for little rulers who operate by tiny motives, meager objectives, belittling goals, silly prejudices, and partial successes. That is why God never sent out an army of men against Rameses II. Because Pharaoh was little, God called a series of armies of little plagues—frogs, lice, sores, locusts, darkness, and disastrous hail. Every option was exhausted to no avail.

From then on, God himself took over. He personally took charge on the night of the Passover by smiting "all the firstborn in the land of Egypt, both man and beast; and against all the gods of Egypt I will execute judgment: I am the Lord" (Exodus 12:12, KJV).

Single-handedly, the I AM THAT I AM waged a battle against Pharaoh and the gods of Egypt. "And it came to pass the selfsame day, that the Lord did bring the children of Israel out of the land of Egypt . . ." (Exodus 12:5, KJV).

After the Hebrews departed and had gotten as far as the Red Sea, Pharaoh's army was sent to return them to Egypt. The Lord divided the waters, and the Israelites went through the path of the sea dry-shod. "And the Egyptians pursued, and went in after them to the midst of the sea, even all Pharaoh's horses, his chariots, and his horsemen" (Exodus 14:23, KJV).

"And it came to pass, that in the morning watch the Lord looked unto the host of the Egyptians through the pillar of fire and of the cloud. . . . And took off their chariot wheels. . . . And the Lord said unto Moses, Stretch out thine hand over the sea. . . . And Moses stretched forth his hand over the sea. . . . And the waters returned, and covered the chariots, and the horsemen, and all the host of Pharaoh that came into the sea after them; there remained not so much as one of them" (Exodus 14:24-28, KJV).

This is a lesson for America. For more than three centuries, God has placed at our disposal many options to liberate black people, poor whites, and others from inequality and injustices. We cannot keep stalling on such an undying issue as freedom. We cannot forever pigeonhole live people who refuse to die until they enjoy equality and the fruits of democracy in this country. Their liberation and security are all tied up with heavenly concerns. If we do not untie them, then they will tie up the nation. When this option is exhausted, perhaps God himself will intervene and rip us, wreck us, and consign us to the junk pile of fallen empires and bankrupt nations.

It may be that our options have not expired. Perhaps this so-called land of the brave and home of the free will pull off its racist cloak of cowardice and operate our national wheels according to a government as ordained of God. Then once more the morning stars shall sing together and the sons of God shall shout for joy.

Benjamin E. Mays was for many years the president of Morehouse College in Atlanta, Georgia. Born in South Carolina, he did his undergraduate work at Bates College in Lewiston, Maine. He earned the Master of Arts degree and the Ph.D. degree from the University of Chicago. He has received honorary degrees from a great number of colleges and universities in the United States, Liberia, and Nigeria. He is president of the Atlanta Board of Education and has served as consultant to the Office of Education in the Department of Health, Education and Welfare, and to the Ford Foundation. He is the author of several books and many articles in magazines and journals.

WHAT MAN LIVES BY
Benjamin E. Mays

Some nineteen centuries ago a Palestinian Jew made these words immortal: "Man shall not live by bread alone, but by every word that proceedeth out of the mouth of God" (Matthew 4:4, KJV). To state it another way: Man shall not live by bread alone but by every good thing that God provides. Man can *exist* on food, air, and water, just as animals can, but man must have more than bread in order to live creatively and constructively.

It is not too much to translate this passage by saying, "Man shall not live by material things alone. Money, houses and land, stocks and bonds, silver and gold, iron and ore, silks and diamonds and pearls and furs are all important, but man may have all these and merely exist—not live."

Jesus stated it wisely: Man shall not live by bread alone. He knew that bread—food—is basic to man's life. And the Devil knew that when a man gets hungry, he is vulnerable and may do many abnormal things in order to get food. Facing starvation, most people would steal, if they could, rather than starve. Using bread as a symbol for food, adequate food for all mankind has been a problem since the beginning of time. It is a crucial problem today. It is estimated that half the people of the earth are starving for lack of bread. Bread is so important that if food became too scarce, the strong man would turn on the weak man and cannibalize him in order to survive. The population explosion threat is no idle dream. If bread becomes too unobtainable, we have the basis for revolution. In man's quest for more bread—more food—and a higher standard of living, labor strikes against management and the common people rise up against the establishment. Those of us who care are appalled by the fact that easily thirty million Americans are living below the poverty line. Bread is important, and man cannot exist without it. But if man had only food, only material things, to live by, he would cease to be a man.

So Jesus says to the Devil that man cannot live by bread alone. If he could, he would be a mere animal. Bread is the means, not the end. Man lives in God, and the circumference of life cannot be rightly drawn until the center is set. Carlyle said that "not all the finance ministers and upholsterers and confectioners of modern Europe in joint stock company" could "make one shoeblack happy . . . above an hour or two." If bread and material things were the *sine qua non* of life, the rich and the affluent would be eternally happy and the less rich would be eternally miserable. But history records, and experience reveals, that some of the most miserable people are among those who have great wealth and those who have achieved fame.

The experience of Jesus in the wilderness is common to all mankind. Simply put, Jesus is trying to decide the basic question that confronts every man: What shall I do with my life? This question faces every man: What shall I do with my life? Although I shall deal with only one of the three temptations, Jesus is getting his priorities straight. Man has to decide what he will put first in his life. This problem faces the young with terrific force. If it is money, material wealth, houses and land, stocks and bonds, silver and gold—as important as these are—if these are central in our lives, human values become secondary. Man may exist, but he will never know the full joy of living. As indispensable as bread is, as vital as material things are, possessions alone have never made a man great. The rich man who achieves a degree of greatness achieves it not because he hoards his wealth but because he gives it away in the interest of good causes—his concern for humanity, his concern for the poor, and his desire to improve the quality of education. The truly great men of history are great not because of the abundance of the things they possessed but because of their dreams and the contributions they made to mankind. It is because they recognized that man cannot live by bread alone.

Many years ago, H. G. Wells named the six great men of history. He named Buddha and Asoka, brown men; Aristotle, a Greek; Roger Bacon, an Englishman; Abraham Lincoln, an American; and the greatest among them, Jesus, a Jew. If I were to name my list, I would want to include men like Albert Schweitzer, Mahatma Gandhi, and my pupil and friend, Martin Luther King, Jr. These men knew that man cannot live by bread alone but by every word that proceedeth out of the mouth of God.

Bread is vital; it is indispensable; but in appraising a man for greatness, wealth per se is never a criterion. Nobody stops to ask how much wealth persons like Fred Douglass, Harriet Tubman, Thomas Aquinas, Albert Einstein, Booker T. Washington, Mary McLeod Bethune, Shakespeare, and Socrates had when they died. They achieved historical immortality long after bread ceased to sustain their bodies. If man cannot live by bread alone, what else does he need to live by? Jesus answers this by saying: By every word that proceedeth out of the mouth of God.

Any man or woman who has a family knows that man lives by affection and love. There may be material things galore, but if there is no affection, no love in the home, the family falls apart. The baby may have all the food it needs, all the air and sunshine, all the protection from cold and heat; yet if he does not get his mother's kisses, her affectionate hugs, her inviting smiles, and her soothing words when he cries, the baby may exist but he will be an abnormal child. The baby must be made to know that he or she is wanted. The child must have the love of father, mother, sisters, and brothers, and the protection they give—all these the child must receive in order to live and flourish.

No man has ever made his wife really happy merely by giving her an abundance of material things. He may give her gold and silver, diamonds and pearls, houses and land, stocks and bonds— all these she will reject if her husband withholds his love. In truth, love is the thing no man and no woman can live without. Affection and love hold the family together; hatred and infidelity tear the family apart. Man cannot live by bread alone. Bread must be accompanied by love and affection.

No man can live without forgiveness. The family cannot hold together without it. The husband and wife must forgive each other for the unkind words they sometimes say to each other, for the unpleasant glances they sometimes give, for being impatient with one another. Even if at times husband and wife are deliberately mean toward one another, they must forgive. Forgiveness is the very essence of happiness in the home. The family cannot survive if the wife seeks opportunities to get revenge for unkind things the husband says and does to her. Nor can the family hold together if the husband seeks retaliation against the wife. Forgiveness is the heart of family life. The father must forgive the son, the son the father; the sister must forgive the brother and the brother the sister; the wife must forgive the husband and the husband the wife. I have even known cases where there was forgiveness where infidelity was involved. It takes a lot of forgiveness to keep a family together.

Man must live by forgiveness, not only family forgiveness but community forgiveness. The prisoner who has served his time needs community forgiveness. Man needs forgiveness for the dirty, vicious things that some do to others. How often have we in some little or big way trespassed against a brother? We live by forgiveness of those friends who love us and stick with us though we sin against them.

But most of all, we live by the forgiveness of God. No man is perfect enough, no man is good enough not to need the forgiveness of God. In one sense we are all sinners. If a sinner is one who sins, we all qualify as sinners. All of us sometimes sin. If it is true that when we sin against man, we sin against God; when we lie to man, we lie to God; when we exploit man, we exploit God; when we hate man, we hate God; God must indeed be a forgiving God with man sinning against him all of the time! Man shall not live by bread alone, but man shall live and does live by the forgiveness of a merciful God.

In addition to bread, man lives by the grace of God. One definition of grace is that we get what we do not deserve. Every man who is honest with himself knows of instances when he got what he did not deserve, certainly that which he did nothing to achieve. God sends his rain on the just and the unjust. The moon and the sun shine on us all. The unrighteous lives as long as the righteous. The best man does not always get the job. We often get honors and prizes which we have not earned. Someone dies and leaves us a bit of wealth which we never turned a little finger to get. The man we do not like sometimes does us a favor, to our embarrassment. We inherit a good mind by some means we do not understand, a mind which we did nothing to get. We develop into a handsome boy or a beautiful girl by nature and nature's God, but we did nothing to get the beauty or the comeliness. Some are born into better circumstances than others, but we are not responsible for where we are born nor for what we are born with. In some degree, we all get what we do not deserve, and we live by the grace of God.

Man shall not live by bread alone. Man must live by faith— faith in himself and faith in others. However beastly man may be, we must believe in him and rely on him. We trust the doctor to operate on our bodies. We trust the man who drives the automobile. We trust the banks to keep our money. We trust the man who directs us to an unfamiliar place. We trust the pilot who takes us three thousand feet above the ground. We live by faith in others. But most of all we must live by faith in ourselves —faith to believe that we can develop into useful men and women. No man can live without faith in himself—a sense of inner security. A child must learn early to believe that he is somebody worthwhile and that he can do many praiseworthy things. Without this hope, there would be nothing for him to do but to commit suicide. Furthermore, man could not live hopefully without believing that he counts for something in this world. The greatest damage that the white man did to the black man through slavery and segregation was to beat him down so much that millions of Negroes believed that they were nobody. The hopelessness and despair of so many black youths today lie in the fact that they have never believed that they have dignity and worth as human beings. If the emphasis on blackness and black awareness today means that black people are beginning to be proud of their heritage and proud of being what they are—black—apologizing to no one—not even to God—for what they are, it is a good thing. Man lives best by a belief that he is somebody, God's creature, and that he has status not given to him by man but given to him by God.

Man must believe that however hard the road, however difficult today, tomorrow things will be better. Tomorrow may not be better, but we must believe that it will be. Wars may never cease, but we must continue to strive to eliminate them. We may not abolish poverty, but we must believe that we can provide bread enough and to spare for every living creature and that we can find the means to distribute it. We may not exterminate racism, but we must believe that different racial groups can live together in peace, and we must never cease to try to build a society in which the fatherhood of God and the brotherhood of man become realities.

In other words, man must live by faith in God—faith to believe that God sustains good and not evil, peace and not war, truth and not lies, justice and not injustice, integrity and not dishonesty, the faith that Browning talks about when he says: [1]

> One who never turned his back but marched breast forward,
>   Never doubted that clouds would break,
> Never dreamed, though right were worsted, wrong would triumph,
> Held we fall to rise, are baffled to fight better,
>   Sleep to wake.

Not by bread alone but by the labors of others. No man is self-sustaining. We are dependent on the labors of many hands for the food we eat, for the clothes we wear, for the cars and planes in which we ride, for the books we read, for the teachers who teach us, for the skill of the surgeon, for the technical training of the pilot. We are dependent on the postman who brings the mail, on the controllers who guide the planes in and out of airports, and on the sanitation workers who take away the garbage.

---

[1] Robert Browning, "Epilogue," *Masterpieces of Religious Verse* (New York: Harper & Row, Publishers, 1948), no. 1863.

Our lives are interlaced, interwoven, and intertwined with the lives of all classes of men, and whether we like it or not we all need each other and every man is our brother.

Man shall not live by bread alone, but man must live by his dreams, by the goals he strives to reach, and by the ideals which he chooses and chases. What is man anyway? Man is flesh and blood, body and mind, bones and muscle, arms and legs, heart and soul, lungs and liver, nerves and veins—all these and more make a man. But man is really what his dreams are. Man is what he aspires to be. He is the ideals that beckon him on. Man is the integrity that keeps him steadfast, honest, true. If a young man tells me what he aspires to be, I can almost predict his future.

It must be borne in mind, however, that the tragedy in life does not lie in not reaching your goal. The tragedy lies in having no goal to reach. It isn't a calamity to die with dreams unfulfilled, but it is a calamity not to dream. It is not a disaster to be unable to capture your ideal, but it is a disaster to have no ideal to capture. It is not a disgrace not to reach the stars, but it is a disgrace to have no stars to reach for. Not failure, but low aim is the sin. Harriet du Autermont has beautifully said: [2]

> No vision and you perish;
> No ideal, and you're lost;
> Your heart must ever cherish
> Some faith at any cost.

> Some hope, some dream to cling to,
> Some rainbow in the sky,
> Some melody to sing to,
> Some service that is high.

To state it another way, man must live by some unattainable goal, some goal that beckons him on, but a goal so lofty, so all-embracing that it can never be attained. In poetry it is expressed in many ways. Browning expresses it when speaking of Andrea del Sarto:

> Ah, but a man's reach should exceed his grasp,
> Or what's a heaven for?

[2] Harriet du Autermont, "Some Faith at Any Cost," *Masterpieces of Religious Verse* (New York: Harper & Row, Publishers, 1948), p. 967.

Lowell says it in his "L'Envoi to the Muse": [3]

Just, just beyond, forever burn
Gleams of a grace without return;
Upon thy shade I plant my foot,
And through my frame strange raptures shoot;

All of thee but thyself I grasp;
I seem to fold thy luring shape,
And vague air to my bosom clasp,
Thou lithe, perpetual Escape!

The unattainable ideal is beautifully expressed by Emerson in his "Forerunners": [4]

Long I followed happy guides,
I could never reach their sides;
Their step is forth, and, ere the day
Breaks up their leaguer, and away.
Keen my sense, my heart was young,
Right good-will my sinews strung,
But no speed of mine avails
To hunt upon their shining trails.
On and away, their hasting feet
Make the morning proud and sweet;
Flowers they strew,—I catch the scent;
Or tone of silver instrument
Leaves on the wind melodious trace;
Yet, I could never see their face.

Untermeyer says it best in his poem "Prayer": [5]

God, though this life is but a wraith,
Although we know not what we use,
Although we grope with little faith,
Give me the heart to fight—and lose.

Ever insurgent let me be,
Make me more daring than devout;

[3] James Russell Lowell, "L'Envoi to the Muse," *The Complete Poetical Works of James Russell Lowell*, Cambridge Edition (Boston: Houghton, Mifflin Company, 1896), pp. 347-348.

[4] Ralph Waldo Emerson, "Forerunners," *Great Poems of the English Language* (New York: Tudor Publishing Co., 1935), p. 663. Used by permission of Houghton Mifflin Company.

[5] Louis Untermeyer, "Prayer," *Long Feud: Selected Poems* (New York: Harcourt Brace Jovanovich, Inc., 1962). Used by permission.

From sleek contentment keep me free,
And fill me with a buoyant doubt.

Open my eyes to visions girt
With beauty, and with wonders lit—
But let me always see the dirt,
And all that spawn and die in it.

Open my ears to music; let
Me thrill with Spring's first flutes and drums—
But never let me dare forget
The bitter ballads of the slums.

From compromise and things half-done,
Keep me, with stern and stubborn pride;
And when, at last, the fight is won,
God, keep me still unsatisfied.

Man shall not live by bread alone. Man must live by affection and love; by forgiveness, forgiveness of man and the forgiveness of God; by God's grace, by the labors of many hands; by faith, faith in himself, faith in others, and by faith in God. And finally man must live by his dreams, his ideals, the unattainable goal, and what he aspires to be. Man shall not live by bread alone.

Samuel B. McKinney is pastor of the Mount Zion Baptist Church in Seattle, Washington. He was born in Cleveland, Ohio. He did his undergraduate work at Morehouse College in Atlanta, Georgia, and earned the B.D. degree from Colgate Rochester Divinity School in Rochester, New York. Linfield College in McMinnville, Oregon, has honored him with the Doctor of Divinity degree. He is a life member of N.A.A.C.P., a member of the national and regional boards of O.I.C., a member of the board of American Baptist Home Mission Societies, and a board member of the National Committee of Black Churchmen, in addition to many other responsibilities.

THE HOT WINDS OF CHANGE
Samuel B. McKinney

Those who observe the liturgical calendar will note that Pentecost Sunday often comes in May. Those troubled by the unheeded "Kerner Report," which stated that our nation is becoming two nations, one white and one black and unequal, will also note that May 17 marks the anniversary of the Supreme Court decision of 1954. This decision declared that public education in the nation could not be separate and equal at the same time.

So this day in May is fraught with significant meaning. And on such a day, Pentecost, fifty days after the sabbath following the Passover—Pentecost, the day when God's spirit permeated one hundred twenty believers and three thousand souls were added to the church—on such a day, May 17, when desegregation of schools has moved ever so slowly and "with all deliberate speed" has given way to "benign neglect," polarization of people in our nation is real and dangerous.

Is there a relationship between the meaning of Pentecost and the anniversary of the Supreme Court decision of May 17, 1954? The hot winds of change are blowing through this nation and world, toppling old systems, challenging all establishments, and calling into question everything considered sacrosanct. Easy answers and solutions to complex questions and problems will not suffice. Where then can we turn for a glimmer of hope and direction? The experience of Pentecost has possibilities worthy of exploration.

I

PENTECOST

Pentecost was one of the three major feasts of the year along with the Feasts of the Tabernacles and the Passover. Following the Passover Feast, attended mainly by Palestinian Jews, at which time Jesus was murdered, the population of Jerusalem returned to normal size. But at Pentecost, with fair weather beckoning, pilgrims poured into the Holy City from all points of the Roman Empire.

Almost unnoticed by the jostling bands of pilgrims, the remnant of Jesus' followers waited. And suddenly it happened—the Spirit came, like a wind, uncontrollable, mysterious, powerful; like a flame, cleansing, consuming, awesome, and dangerous. The small band of one hundred twenty was gathered in the same place, and the Spirit was given to the entire group, resting upon each of them.

Was this the first time the Spirit of God had come upon men? No! What unique thing transpired at Pentecost? The Spirit of God was made manifest in a new way. The Spirit, which was at work in Creation, fell upon the leaders and the prophets of Israel, but never in the Old Testament was the Spirit poured out upon all the people. When it was poured out, only the leaders received it and then just enough to make them desire more. Moses cried aloud, "Would God that all the Lord's people were prophets, and that the Lord would put his spirit upon them!" (Numbers 11:29, KJV). Isaiah hoped the Messiah would be different because the Spirit would rest upon him.

Ezekiel wondered, "Can these bones live?" And the answer came, "If the breath of the Lord breathes upon them." Joel longed for the day when the Spirit would be poured out upon all flesh, not just upon a few leaders but on all (Joel 2:28-29, KJV).

In his hometown of Nazareth, Jesus turned to the prophecy of Isaiah and announced in no uncertain terms what has become the Christian's Manifesto of Liberation,

> The Spirit of the Lord God is upon me;
> Because the Lord hath anointed me
> To preach good tidings unto the meek;
> He hath sent me to bind up the brokenhearted,
> To proclaim liberty to the captives,
> And the opening of the prison to them that are bound;
> To proclaim the acceptable year of the Lord,
> And the day of vengeance of our God;
> To comfort all that mourn . . .
> To give unto them beauty for ashes,
> The oil of joy for mourning,
> The garment of praise for the spirit of heaviness.
>
> Isaiah 61:1-3 (KJV)

The longings of the Old Testament were fulfilled on the day of Pentecost, for the Lord's Spirit was poured out on the entire assembly. This says to us that God is not dead but very much alive and at work in history and in the universe. In fact, it has been rumored in some places that when it was discovered that God was a "black woman," white theologians declared God dead. A new Israel is being formed; a new Israel which takes the burning bush experience of one man and superimposes it as "cloven tongues of fire" upon one hundred twenty; a new Israel which transforms a harvest feast into a harvest of three thousand souls; a new Israel, which looks back to the Law given fifty days after the deliverance from Egypt and sees in the descent of the Holy Spirit, fifty days after the resurrection of Jesus Christ, the mighty redemptive act without parallel.

This mighty act of redemption was not only the launching pad of the church, but it suggests that Pentecost is not a thing apart from daily life nor God's divine purpose in history. In Pentecost we see the Spirit of the Eternal fashioning, molding, and making a new people by using the "hot winds of change" in a creative manner. In Pentecost we see the breath of God energizing his children and making the dead bones of hope and promise live again. The church, established by the "winds of God," was marked by a new quality of life, a society of love, joy, and hope. We see in Pentecost the Spirit of the Eternal actively leading his people in all truth.

II

THE HOPE OF A NEW AGE

My Bible tells me when men tried to make a name for themselves by building a tower to the heavens, God confused their language. But in the day of Pentecost a new age is born when men of all nations are made over into the people of God. As the nursery rhyme lilts:

> Humpty Dumpty sat on a wall,
> Humpty Dumpty had a great fall;
> All the king's horses and all the king's men
> Couldn't put Humpty together again.

The ancient breach made among men at the Tower of Babel was healed by the gift of the Spirit. At Pentecost, God put his people back together again.

With thousands hungry for a crumb of hope, the message of Jesus spread throughout the ancient world. Where it was received, a new creature in Christ was born and had to be nourished. When this new creature applied his religion to life, things began to happen. Old orthodoxies, traditions, and customs were challenged. Because the challengers of the status quo felt compelled to make relevant their witness because of the earthshaking, mind-blowing, life-transforming experience of their Pentecost, repression, suppression, and backlash became real. Persecution, suffering, and tribulation became their lot. Somehow these heroes of the faith "forgot themselves into immortality" because they sensed they were on the threshold of a new day.

On the seventeenth day of May in 1954 the United States Supreme Court took a fresh look at an old problem and by law struck the death knell for segregation in education. The Supreme Court looked beyond the mere legalistic view or strict constructionist view and took into consideration the morality and sociology of the situation. In essence they discovered what we must all recognize, that injustice anywhere can lead to injustice everywhere; blind hatred and bigotry anywhere can lead to blind hatred and bigotry everywhere. If America was to maintain its role as moral leader of the world, it had to set its house in order.

Today we find people more divided, separated, segregated, re-segregated, polarized, uptight, revealing the brokenness of our contemporary society. The anniversary of the May 17, 1954, Supreme Court decision signifies that America can still have a "birth of freedom" and the dream smoldering in the bosom of the black man *must* become a reality *now!* The vision of this nation, under God, will come to fruition when "all flesh shall see it together," for a divided America is doomed.

Pentecost was a reversal of Babel. Dr. Colin W. Williams has said: "The Tower of Babel story shows men grasping at God's prerogatives and storming the citadel of heaven with the work of their own hands. The result of this proud attempt of men is many tongues and myriad nations.

"Man, by turning away from the one God, condemned himself to life behind the dividing walls of his own partial communities. But at Pentecost, the power of God's Spirit breached the walls of partition, and the church is given to the world as God's new creation. Here is a community in which barriers of language and nation are overcome, for out of the many the Spirit makes one new man in Jesus Christ."

I submit to you, however, that Richard M. Nixon, president of the United States, has attempted to reverse Pentecost and re-institute Babel. With the cacophony of noise emanating from the White House and with the muting of all trumpets of hope, we need to have the ceiling raised on the legitimate aspirations of the people whose backs are against the wall. Mr. Nixon said to black America, "Judge us not by our rhetoric but by our deeds." The deeds of the Nixon administration make it crystal clear to black America what to expect—absolutely nothing of substance. Not only is black America in trouble but all America is in trouble. The Nixon administration has declared war on students, poor people, disinherited people, disenfranchised people, educated people, and people sensitive to America's involvement as *"Daddy Warbucks"* to the world and *"Buck Rogers"* in outer space.

Somehow the cries of pain are not heard, and many young people feel compelled to attempt almost anything to gain the attention of the president and his staff. Mr. Nixon is receiving bad advice, but he has done nothing to remedy the situation.

It appears that the *new Babel* will consist of a society where only the so-called silent majority is heard from and the minorities might be listened to but not heeded. The new Babel, southern strategy, would encourage a resurgence of White Citizens' Councils, Ku Klux Klans, Know-Nothings, vigilantes from "middle America" to rise up and trample on any liberating and liberalizing tendencies to be found in the nation. The new Babel would attempt to reposition the nation on every issue designed to make the common man's lot better and load easier. The new Babel would attempt to turn back the hands of time and undo everything the "Warren Court" accomplished. The new Babel would not bring us together but do everything in its power to widen the generation gap, the political gap, the social gap, the credibility gap, the sex gap, and all other gaps, instead of trying to bridge all these chasms.

The message of Babel is clear if we would listen. *All attempts on man's part to manipulate people or nature are doomed to failure.* A dominant white male society has for centuries attempted to manipulate its women, black people, and nature. *All of the manipulated are in rebellion.* Western man must now sit down to a banquet of consequences and partake of its just deserts. Nature is rebelling because its very balance is threatened by man's misuse of God's creation. Women are rebelling because they have been used and misused by male whims and desires. Black people, yellow people, brown people, red people, poor white people, and third-world people are in revolt in this nation and around the world because they have been made the pawns of Western man's rape of the universe.

God made man just a little lower than himself and granted him dominion over the earth as his trustee of creation, to make the earth flourish and provide for all men.

Take note, biblical scholars, that the story of Babel appears early in the biblical record, Genesis 11 to be exact, and the Bible ends on the note of a united humanity, dwelling peacefully in the New Jerusalem. *There is no place in today's world, or the world to come, for divisive Babels.* BABEL WILL BE DESTROYED

AND ITS PEOPLE SCATTERED AND THEIR LANGUAGE CONFUSED. The new society in the midst of its present birth pains will have us know that there is no room for fragmentizing tendencies. *In the "New Jerusalem" there is "plenty good room for all God's children."* There must be as much concern for what has transpired at Jackson State College and Augusta, Georgia, as for what happened at Kent State.

III

PENTECOST AND YOU

Pentecost is God's reversal of Babel and the church's mission to be the sign of that reversal. Pentecost calls for a new nation and a new people. You must help create a new nation by becoming a new people.

The hot winds of change blowing through the world are forcing us to search again in the Book of Books for hope. Colin Williams reminds us that the new community brought into being by Pentecost could sing with the apostle Paul: "In Christ there is no Greek nor Jew [national and racial barriers are overcome in Christ]; no bond or free [class barriers fall]; no barbarian or Scythian [cultural barriers, too, are transcended]; no male or female [distinctions based on sex also are broken down], for all are one in him. Here at Pentecost we are given the one family of God, the New Humanity."

The "New Humanity" places certain demands on those who take it seriously. What is expected of a new people? A new people must open themselves to the hot winds of change so that they might be instruments in the hands of the Eternal to eradicate from the earth the problems of white racism, poverty, hunger, disease, pollution, and war. A new humanity must endeavor to help all men realize what was experienced in the days of King Solomon: "And Judah and Israel dwelt safely, every man under his vine and under his fig tree, from Dan even to Beer-sheba . . ." (1 Kings 4:25, KJV).

A "New People" must also participate, helping to harmonize man and nature. Here is the dream of the prophet Isaiah as we read it in the Bible. God depends on people like you and me to see to it that it comes to pass:

The wolf also shall dwell with the lamb,
And the leopard shall lie down with the kid;
And the calf and the young lion and the fatling together;
And a little child shall lead them,
And the cow and the bear shall feed;
Their young ones shall lie down together;
And the lion shall eat straw like the ox;
And the sucking child shall play on the hole of the asp;
And the weaned child put his hand on the cockatrice' den.
They shall not hurt nor destroy
    in all my holy mountain:
For the earth shall be full of the knowledge of the Lord,
As the waters cover the sea.

Isaiah 11:6-9 (KJV)

A new people must project a new ideal for man and society.

A new people, a new humanity, brought together by the hot winds of change, must be blessed with the gift of articulation. On the day of Pentecost, a man, rough in exterior, gentle in heart, a fisherman by trade, a natural leader, but no orator by any stretch of the imagination, was touched by the Eternal Spirit which cut loose his stammering, God-denying tongue, and such as needed to be saved were added to the church. Just as Simon Peter was made a flaming evangelist and a martyr, so God's Spirit, resting upon us, can transform our average, meager, mediocre talents into superlative attributes.

The power which moved upon the face of the deep and brought order out of chaos, something out of nothingness, is available today. The power which sent Abraham out of the security of his homeland in search of a city whose maker and builder is God is available today. The power which returned Moses, a fugitive from justice as the liberator of his kindred, will release God's people today. The power which set on hallowed fire people like Elijah, Elisha, Isaiah, Jeremiah, Micah, Amos, and Hosea can set us on fire for the cause of justice and righteousness. The Spirit which became a heavy burden on Ezra and Nehemiah will rest as a wearisome load upon us when we see the desolation and waste of potential all about us. The Spirit which could cause a Saul to make a U turn on the Damascus Road and become the apostle Paul, the greatest Christian missionary, can turn men around and start them in the right direction, for God is in the business of rescuing priceless treasures from the junk heaps of life's wreckage. This same power which enabled a Martin Luther to stand upon the truth revealed in God's word is available to stand men upon their feet when assailed by the self-appointed guardians of the status quo.

The hot winds of change, blowing through the central city ghettos of just about every major city, are producing an articulate group of young people whose rhetoric may possess the seeds of hope for tomorrow and enable all of us to develop a theology of revolution needed for the foreseeable future. These young people, out of their purifying black experience, are developing their own pantheon of heroes, including Martin Luther King, Jr., Malcolm X, Eldridge Cleaver, Muhammed Ali, James Brown, Jesse Jackson, and others. Just about all of these men have defied white racist structures in their lives and have found their salvation in resisting and overcoming barriers placed in their paths. The verbalization of their plight has helped to motivate many white youth who wish to join a struggle to set all men free. Dr. Vincent Harding, of the Institute of the Black World, of Atlanta, Georgia, suggests that young black men today are embarked on a quest *to define manhood in our times, to understand the black man's plight as a colonized people in an hostile environment, to change their names as a symbol of divesting themselves of a slave mentality, and to make sure that all institutions discover, study, and revere the "Black Fathers" in the same way black America knows all about the white fathers.*

A professor at the University of Washington said, after Dr. Martin Luther King's assassination, that the real earthshaking revolution will sweep this nation when the white youth from affluent families become weary of their "good life" and cast their lot with the dispossessed and "wretched of the earth." The hot winds of change will enable you to throw off your weight of powerlessness and, with newfound powers of articulation, be the advocate of the disinherited of the world.

The prophet Jeremiah deemed it necessary to root up, tear down, and destroy the dehumanizing structures of his day. Wisdom also dictated that he plant and build a new order. What kind of world do you plan to build? How do you define manhood today? Are you in the process of acquiring a new name and a new nature? The hot winds of change enabled the apostle Paul to proclaim that in Christ we become new creatures, a new creation.

Babel personifies the entombment of values, culture, ideals, and what is considered "the good." Pentecost stands for liberation, the releasing of all that has been locked up, jailed, repressed, or suppressed. Babel means death. Pentecost means life. The hot winds of change are blowing through the land. "I tell you, it's blowing in the wind."

Change will occur whether we desire it or not. A friend of mine tells of standing before the majestic Sphinx and the great Pyramids of Egypt. On one hand, he felt like Napoleon Bonaparte who, on viewing the same scene centuries earlier, said to his troops, "The centuries are looking down on you." On the other hand, my friend remembered that pieces of granite the size of boxcars were fitted together by slave labor to construct these wonders of the world. But over the years the hot winds of the desert have been defacing and chipping away at the mighty works of ancient Egyptian monarchs who thought they could secure immortality and posterity for themselves. They entombed in Babel what they considered "the good," but today it is simply a tourist site.

Not too far away from Egypt lived a man who built no mighty monuments in granite, brick, and stone, but whose spirit, enflamed with the hot winds of the Eternal, turned the world upside down, put it right side up, and indelibly etched God's love upon the hearts of millions: Jesus of Nazareth, the lowly carpenter's son, whose matchless words, whose peerless deeds, whose untimely death, whose liberating resurrection, and whose validating Pentecost has a message for us today.

He would say to us in essence that the Spirit of the living God, the hot winds of change, must set our tongues aflame for justice, must strangely warm our hearts anew on the altar of compassion for all men, and must translate our articulation into concrete visceral actions to release men to be themselves.

When be become ourselves again, then the words of Jesus will have greater impact: "Inasmuch as you have done it to the least of these, you have done it to me."

I dare you to open yourself to the hot winds of God today—right now!

Otis Moss, Jr., is pastor of the Mount Zion Baptist Church in Lockland, Ohio. He formerly served as co-pastor of the Ebenezer Baptist Church in Atlanta, Georgia, with Dr. M. L. King, Sr. A native of Georgia, he earned the A.B. and B.D. degrees at Morehouse College and School of Religion in Atlanta. He has also taken additional work at the Inter-Denominational Theological Center in Atlanta. He is a national board member of the Southern Christian Leadership Conference and the Martin Luther King, Jr., Center, where he is also a trustee. He has served with local boards of the N.A.A.C.P. and O.I.C. In 1967 he was named as one of "the most outstanding young men of America." He is currently a member of the board of directors of PUSH (People United to Save Humanity).

GOING FROM DISGRACE TO DIGNITY
Otis Moss, Jr.

Then they went out to see what was done; and came to Jesus, and found the man, out of whom the devils were departed, sitting at the feet of Jesus, clothed, and in his right mind: and they were afraid.
Luke 8:35 (KJV)

"Going from disgrace to dignity." I think this has been the purpose of the black church in history, for the "Middle Passage" (slave trade) was such a disgraceful chapter in human history that some people denied that it ever existed. Some people rewrote the history of slavery and said it was a benevolent enterprise. Others attached a serious footnote to the pages of history and said that the black cargo from West Africa to North America was after all a rescue mission: it rescued the black man from the jungles of a cannibalistic Africa and put him on the road to civilization. How can an uncivilized inhuman act put another man on the road to civilization? But this is what some historians would have us to believe. I went to the University of Cincinnati bookstore a few months ago and bought two volumes on *The History of Civilization.* Less than fifty pages were on Africa, and yet it was entitled *The History of Civilization! That* is disgraceful, and our mission, our purpose, our calling, our commitment, our charge in this present age is to move from disgrace to dignity. When the movement is a reality, it stirs a concern in the community and people will go out to see what's happening. They went out to see what was done. Now pause at that section of the verse which says, "they went out to *see* what was done." They didn't go out to learn, just to see. They didn't go out to appreciate, but to see. They didn't go out to participate or to become involved, but to see. And here is where the line is drawn between the role we play in life and history.

Some people become and remain eternal spectators; they just go out to see. You can see them standing on the sidelines of every demonstration in history; they just want to see. They even come to church that way. They can tell you when the organist didn't strike the right key; they can tell you whose hat and shoes didn't match—they just see. They can tell you whose subject and verb didn't agree—they're not concerned about the reality of communication. I have a colleague in the ministry who often says, "If another man says to you, 'I *is* going kill you,' I think you will get the message!" Even though the grammatical construction of his statement may not be according to Anglo-Saxon standards, the reality of the power behind what he said might start some changes in your mind and feet. And the challenge is: "Where will I stand in life; where will I stand under the conditions of existence; where will I stand in history? As an eternal spectator or as a participant?" "Then they went out to see what was done."

Now the evangelist underscores three conditions about the man he was speaking of: "at the feet of Jesus," an indication that he had some poise and coordination and he had reverence; "sitting at the feet of Jesus, clothed," he was not naked, symbolically or otherwise. He had dignity. ". . . clothed and in his right mind," he was "together." He had wholeness; he had integrity. Then the writer opens a wide door on the conditions of the community where the man lived, ". . . and they were afraid." Now isn't it interesting that that statement comes *after* the description of the man's condition and experience? That ". . . [he was] sitting at the feet of Jesus, clothed, and in his right mind: and *they were afraid,*" is an indication that while the man was torn apart, while he was naked without integrity, while he was not together, while he was without his clothes, when he didn't know Jesus, didn't know himself, and didn't know his brother, nobody was too concerned about him. The community adjusted to the fact that he was consigned to perpetual irrelevance. But when they found him dressed up, when they found him hanging around Jesus, when they found him "together," *they were afraid.*

I see a black and white parallel here. As long as we were struggling in the cotton fields of Tennessee, Georgia, Alabama, and Mississippi with cotton sacks across our shoulders and to our sides, picking cotton and having our fingers burning from stinging cotton worms that would hide under the cotton leaves; as long as we were barefoot, actually and symbolically, laughing when we were not tickled. (No, we were not laughing; we were grinning. If I were giving a lecture in black psychology, I would tell you the difference between a laugh and a grin. A laugh comes from the inside and is an expression of joyous fulfillment, but a grin comes from the outside and is a sign of defense); as long as we were saying "yas, sir, and yas, ma'am," when we really meant "hell no!" As long as we were in that bag tied up with Christmas paper with a symbol of Santa Claus on it (and he was white), America was satisfied. But one day America looked up and saw us standing before the Supreme Court interpreting the Constitution much better than those who wrote it, without the contradictions in our lives that Washington and Jefferson had in theirs. After the Revolutionary War was over, George Washington, rather than trying to build a free nation, was up in New York looking for his runaway slaves. Patrick Henry said, "Give me liberty or give me death," but he had slaves when he made the statement. I've often wondered what would have happened when Patrick Henry said, "Give me liberty or give me death," if one of his slaves had stood up and said, "Me, too!"

But one day America saw us marching to the voting booth,

sitting down at lunch counters, and all of America became afraid, and as the movement continued, every community in this nation found it necessary to draw up new appropriations for police equipment. They started training men how to shoot better, not to think better. ". . . and [they] found the man, out of whom the devils were departed, sitting at the feet of Jesus, clothed, and in his right mind: and they were afraid."

Let me give you another example. As long as we conceived of Africa, talked about Africa, wrote about Africa, in terms of Tarzan and Jungle Jim or Tarzan and Jane (who never did get married although they spent a lot of time in the woods together, a strange commentary on our puritanical morality), as long as we could think of Africa in that sense, the Western world was happy. As long as Africa could be placed on the balance sheet of Western economics in terms of profit and loss, the West was happy. When England discovered that colonialism was more profitable than slavery and safer, too, England then took the lead to abolish slavery in order to introduce colonialism, gaining in history the reputation of one who became a leading emancipator. And some folks believed it! As long as we could think of Africa in a subhuman sense, the Western world was happy. But one day when we heard the rumblings of Lumumba, the marching feet of Jomo Kenyatta, the sound stretched across Africa and shook the nerve center of the Western world. England and Western civilization had a nervous breakdown—since then we've been trembling. Even the premier of Russia and the president of the United States will step on each other's feet now, in order to have coffee with an African diplomat, not out of love but out of necessity. ". . . and [they] found the man, out of whom the devils were departed, sitting at the feet of Jesus, clothed, and in his right mind: and they were afraid."

What about this man? Well, in the first place, he was lost. Somewhere in his past, I don't know where, somebody cut him off from his roots and he became like, I guess, Elton Trueblood's concept of humanism; he became a "cut flower." He couldn't bear his burdens in the heat of the day, and the world saw the scars on the outside but not the tragedy on the inside. He was lost, inwardly and outwardly. When Jesus asked him, "What is your name?" he came up with a strange response, "My name is Legion, for we are many." Howard Thurman suggests that for a few fleeting moments it rushed through the man's mind, "That's my trouble! I don't know my name. I don't know who I am. There are so many of *me* that I don't know which *me* the real *me* is." My name is Legion! I'm lost. They snatched me from the land of my birth where there was melody and harmony, didn't ask me my name but just gave me a name. I don't know who I am. When you're inwardly lost, the logical question is, "Who am I?" When you're outwardly lost, the logical question is, "Where am I?" This man didn't know who he was, and he didn't know where he was. He was a stranger in a strange land, a poor pilgrim of sorrow. I don't know who I am. Some folks call me "nigger," but that's not my name; some folks call me "boy," and I've already lived three score and ten years; some folks call me "uncle," but they're not my nieces and nephews. My children simply say "him" and my wife just says "that man." Some folks call me "neurotic"; some call me "psychotic"; some call me "crazy"; some call me "foolish"; some call me "low-down"—I don't know who I am. But then the March of Divinity, moving through history, touched the historical moment, and the wings of the angel touched his soul, and somehow spirituality and reality burst out of history and said, "I've got a new name over in Zion. I'm not what you call me. I've got a new name over in Zion. It's mine; I declare it's mine!" The man was lost. Can't you see the parallel here?

Not only was the man lost but he was a sick man, sick unto death. When you are sick unto death, you are drifting and swinging between life and death—too dead to be alive and too alive to be dead—sick unto death. Kierkegaard said that despair is sickness unto death. When you've lost your identity, when you've lost your purpose, when you've lost your hope, when you've lost your integrity, when you've lost your dignity—you are sick unto death. Not only that, but when you destroy another man's dignity, when you've lynched another man's purpose, when you've slaughtered another man's dreams, you are more than sick unto death. You are a murderer guilty of genocide and yet your peers will not charge you as such. When a man is sick, he needs more than a prescription from the corner drugstore. He needs healing, and healing denotes a radical change, and a radical change denotes the end of something, the fulfillment of something, and the beginning of something. That's my definition of revolution.

Not only was the man sick, but the world around him was sick also. Another way of putting it is: he was an insane man in an insane world. The record, in terms of his behavior and his condition and position would give you enough empirical evidence to call him insane or crazy without fear of contradiction, but the world around him was more insane than he was. He was an insane man living in an insane world. I know the community was insane, because the community didn't provide any housing for him. He needed a place to live, but he had to go to the cemetery. He needed a place to learn, but no schoolhouse was available, and it seemed as if the community broke down his altar and he had no altar at which to bow. He needed love, and the community gave him chains—wrapped him up with chains—tied him up and locked him up and then excommunicated him from the human race and criticized him for misbehaving. He was a crazy man in a crazy world.

I want to tell you today, we *still* live in a crazy world. This must be a crazy world. A world that will send a little boy to jail for stealing hub caps from an automobile that was designed to go out of style in less than twelve months after it was made and then give the man who made it the Better Business Award must be a crazy world! Let me bring it home a little closer. A world that will send a child to jail charged with juvenile delinquency for stealing a loaf of bread because he's hungry and then give a man an award for stealing a bank must be a crazy world! A world that will send a man to jail for throwing a brick and then crown a man with honors for stealing a country or a continent must be a crazy world! A world that would assassinate a Martin Luther King, Jr., and then run a George Wallace for president or elect an Agnew vice-president must be a crazy world!

This was a crazy man in a crazy world passing through the valley of disgrace, a valley that all of us sometime or another must pass through. Our foreparents knew this and they said, ". . . you got to walk the lonesome valley, you got to walk it for yourself. Nobody here can walk it for you; you got to walk it for yourself." Nobody is exempt from the valley of disgrace. William James was brilliant, but he contemplated suicide. Harry Emerson Fosdick was a great preacher, but he came home one night with a brilliant academic career behind him, engaged to be married to a wonderful woman, and he said, in his autobiography, that he didn't know what would have happened to him that night as he nervously brought a razor to his throat, but his father kept calling, "Harry, Harry." When you are sick, when you are insane, if somebody close by can keep on calling you by your *right* name, maybe you can find your way.

What happened to the man? He met a revolutionary prophet from the ghetto called Nazareth, whose father, Joseph, couldn't get in the building trades even though he was the best carpenter in town. They said Joseph wasn't qualified. So the man met a preacher from the ghetto. It was so rough in that Nazarene ghetto that everybody declared that nothing good ever came out of Nazareth. But he met this man, a man named Jesus, and Jesus looked at him with love and reached out to him with brotherhood and pulled him in with purpose. Brotherhood, love, and purpose embraced him, and for the first time he felt like a man. For the first time he felt himself able to stand on his feet. Somebody has said that when a man stands erect in the world, only the bottoms of his feet touch the ground and the rest of him will be mingled with the stars, communing with eternity. He met a man named Jesus and something happened in his life.

I can understand why he wanted to stay with Jesus. You would have had the same desire and so would I. Let me stay with you —you, you told me that I'm somebody. Let me stay with you! Something happened to him. What happened to the man? I guess William James would say, "He had reorientation of his personality." I guess E. Stanley Jones would say that he had his "master motive changed." Paul Tillich would say that he was "grasped by an Ultimate Concern." The New Testament would just say that he was born again.

I don't know about you; I can't altogether and adequately define what happened to the man, but I can borrow the language from my foreparents and describe a little bit of what happened. Our foreparents said: "I was on a downward road, no hat on my head, no shoes on my feet, no God on my side, no heaven in my view. Too mean to live and not fit to die. The handcuffs of hell on my hands, the shackles of damnation on my feet, but the Lord spoke peace to my dying soul, turned me around, cut loose my stammering tongue, sent me on my way. And ever since that day, I've been sometimes rising and sometimes falling but I made my vow to the Lord and I'll *never* turn back no more.

I'm going to run on and see what the end's gonna be." The last time that I saw the man he was on his way home. His eyes were clear with sight and insight. His body was straight. The scars of dull and dirty needles had been washed from his body. He was no longer the vehicle of dope but the instrument of hope. The last time that I saw him he was on his way home. His children saw him walking and smiled to themselves and said, "That looks like *my* daddy." His wife looked out and saw him and said, "That's *my* husband." And I can hear the man describing what happened to him. Can't you hear him saying: "I met a man named Jesus, and I had an exchange with him. I gave him my sorrows, he gave me his joy; I gave him my confusion, he gave me his peace; I gave him my despair, he gave me his hope; I gave him my hatred, he gave me his love; I gave him my torn life, he gave me his purpose. I met a man—a man named Jesus. Now I can tell the world, I know I got religion, yes, yes. I know I got religion, yes, yes, and the world can't do me any harm. I have found meaning, purpose, love, and truth, and that makes me a 'New Creation.' "

David T. Shannon is Dean of the Faculty of Pittsburgh Theological Seminary. A native of Virginia, he received his Bachelor of Arts degree from Virginia Union University and the Bachelor of Divinity degree from the School of Religion at the same university. He earned the Master of Sacred Theology degree at Oberlin Graduate School of Theology and has done additional graduate work at Union Theological Seminary, Oxford University, and the Catholic University of America. Before coming to his present position, he was Associate Professor of Religion at Bucknell University in Lewisburg, Pennsylvania. He has also served as a staff member of the American Baptist Board of Education and Publication, a pastor, and visiting professor in several colleges.

A STRANGE SONG IN A STRANGE LAND
David T. Shannon

The black men of Africa, unlike the Israelites of old when they were captured by the Babylonians, were not only able to adapt to their captivity and enslavement in America, but by so doing, they also made a great contribution to the culture of this land that was forced upon them. Although enslaved, they were able to sing a strange song in a strange land. The Israelites, on the other hand, refused to sing when they were captured in a strange land even at the request of their captors. They felt that to sing of their God in a strange land would be sacrilegious. They felt that they were not to sing the songs of their God in a foreign land, as Psalm 137 tells us. But the black man sang, without request, as a confirmation of his belief that his God would help him wherever he was. The work songs of the black African slaves in America, their jazz, and particularly their spirituals—all of which have become absorbed in our American culture—attest to this fact.

After visiting a slave castle in Elmina, Africa, I returned to my hotel room and began reading Psalm 137. The thoughts of the psalm are quite orderly and logical. The psalmist speaks to his condition and that of his fellow exiles as they experienced alienation, loneliness, and dejection while they sat by the river Chebar in Babylon. Their mood was melancholy. Sadness engulfed them. The writer shares this mood with us as he bemoans, "By the waters of Babylon, there we sat down and wept" (Psalm 137:1, RSV). His gloom was deepened by the contrast of how things used to be to the way things were. Recalling the beauty of the past heightened the agony of the present; he continued his self-pity as he wrote, "When we remembered Zion," reflecting upon the joys, the music, the fellowship, and the community of Zion. All that Zion stood for was cast in sharp contrast to the dejection of their situation by the waters of Babylon. In desperation the writer states, "On the willows there we hung up our lyres."

The Israelites' situation was aggravated by their captors who taunted them by asking, "Are these the sweet singers of Israel? Are these the great poets and bards? Are these the musicians of the land of Canaan? Why have they hung up their lyres? Why can't they make music even here in Babylon?" These questions were turned into commands. The writer states:

> For there our captors
> required of us songs,
> and our tormentors, mirth, saying,
> "Sing us one of the songs of Zion!"
> Psalm 137:3 (RSV)

The response of the Israelites to this command is remarkable. It is understandable and expected. They refused to sing! Why? Their reasoning could have been psychological—captivity does not make one wish to sing. Their reasoning could have been musical— their lyres were hung in retirement and had to be tuned. But their reasoning was theological. They did not sing the Lord's song in a strange land, for they believed to do so would be sacrilegious. They asked, "How shall we sing the Lord's song in a foreign land?" They could sing the songs of their Lord in Zion, in a prayer meeting among themselves, in a community of the faithful, but never among strange and hostile people!

But not so the African slaves when they found themselves in a strange land. Contrary to the Israelites, the African slaves believed that perhaps then more than ever, because they were in a foreign land, they needed to sing of and to their God. Instead of making their plight more deplorable through self-pity, as did the Israelites, the black slaves dared to believe that their Lord would free them, somehow, from their captors.

A look at some of the Negro spirituals shows that the songs sung by the black slaves as their response to their American existence can be divided into several categories. Three of these categories—hope, struggle, and overcoming—will be mentioned to illustrate briefly the black slaves' belief in their God.

Two examples of hope grow out of the slaves' songs, one based on the question of Jeremiah and another on the story of the blind man (Luke 18:35-43). Jeremiah, out of agony and despair, asked rhetorical questions: "Is there no balm in Gilead? Is there no physician there?" (Jeremiah 8:22) But the black slaves took the question mark and infused this state of despair with affirmation and hope. The spiritual exchanges the question for an exclamation point. There *is* a balm in Gilead, the spiritual affirms:

> There is a balm in Gilead,
>   To make the wounded whole;
> There is a balm in Gilead,
>   To heal the sin-sick soul.

Hope, based upon a hard realism, is also expressed by the spiritualist who based a song on the story of Jesus' healing the blind man. The biblical story in the Gospel of Luke highlights several motifs: the persistent cry of the blind man, the taunting rejections of the crowd, and the healing by Jesus. The black spiritual writer, however, deals specifically with only one of these motifs—the persistent cry of the blind man. It implies the idea of the crowd's rebuke, but it does not in any way refer to the healing motif—healing with the hope that one day his Lord would make him healed against slavery. He sang:

The blind man stood by the road and cried,
The blind man stood by the road and cried,
The blind man stood by the road and cried
O, Lord, have mercy on me.

Many of the spirituals of the black slaves in America tell of their struggle to be free and their belief that this freedom will come from their God. Miles Mark Fisher, in his book *Negro Slave Songs in the United States,* implies another interesting use by the slaves of their Lord's name—that of a code for the communication networks that existed on the slave plantations. The group of spirituals dealing with the struggle of the slaves suggests a real sensitivity to the life they were living and their willingness to use whatever means necessary to free themselves from this struggle. This category of spirituals can be divided into four groups:

1. To make jest at their masters, they sang such lines as:

Heab'n, heab'n, ev'rybody talkin' 'bout heab'n,
ain't goin' dere,
Heab'n, heab'n, goin' to shout all over God's
heab'n.

2. When they called for a meeting, they sang:

Steal away, steal away,
Steal away to Jesus,
Steal away, steal away home,
I ain't got long to stay here!

3. When some slaves failed to show up for the meeting, they sang:

An' I couldn't hear nobody pray, O Lord,
I couldn't hear nobody pray, O Lord,
O 'way down yonder by myself,
An' I couldn't hear nobody pray.

4. To spread the news among themselves, they sang:

Bad news—

Up above my head I see, Trouble in the air,
Up above my head I see, Trouble in the air,
Up above my head I see, Trouble in the air,
There must be a God somewhere.

Good news—

> Up above my head I hear, Music in the air,
> Up above my head I hear, Music in the air,
> Up above my head I hear, Music in the air,
> There must be a God somewhere.

Thus, the spiritualists captured the struggle of the black slaves in song as they sang of their troubles to and about their God.

A third category of spirituals—overcoming—stressed the motif of "actualized hope." The theological underpinning of hope gave dynamism to the struggle and enabled the slaves to see freedom as a real possibility. For example, when they sang:

> Deep river, my home is over Jordan;
> Deep river, Lord, I want to cross over into campground.

they were symbolically going from bondage to freedom. The words express the slaves' deep desire to overcome servitude and to walk freely in the promised land. To speak of the river as being "deep" was to take into account that overcoming the evils of slavery was not an easy task, but a possible one.[1]

How could the Africans, transported to America as slaves, sing about their God when the Israelites, while they were captured by the Babylonians, could not sing of their God? The Hebrew religion developed externally from the mountain, the tabernacle, the festivals, the temple, and the synagogue. The black slave was forced to develop an internal core as the basis of his religious experience. Circumstances drove him to a style of religion that was dependent upon internal validation and internal authentication. His songs were born of this internalization, which even today manifests itself in what has come to be known as "soul music."

[1] J. Garfield Owens, *All God's Chillun* (Nashville: Abingdon Press, 1971), pp. 23-26.

Kelly Miller Smith is pastor of the First Baptist Church, Capitol Hill, in Nashville, Tennessee. Born in Mississippi, he is a graduate of Morehouse College in Atlanta, and Howard University School of Religion in Washington, D.C. He has taken additional graduate work in Vanderbilt University and Harvard University. At the present time, in addition to his pastoral responsibilities, he is Assistant Dean of Vanderbilt University Divinity School. He has pastored a church in Mississippi and taught at Natchez College and the American Baptist Theological Seminary before coming to his present position. He serves on the boards of Morehouse School of Religion, the American Baptist Foreign Mission Society, the Southern Regional Council, Family and Children's Service, and the Tennessee Council of Churches. In 1954 he was listed as "One of America's Ten Most Outstanding Preachers" by Ebony Magazine, and he has received numerous other honors and citations.

TIME IS WINDING UP!
Kelly Miller Smith

I bring you words which emanated from the wounded and talented bosoms of black, unknown, and unlettered bards of long ago. Although the setting for these words bore a different sociological designation, this application is not an anachronism, for the fare of many in our day may accurately be described as but a variation on the theme of human slavery. Listen to these words:

> Time, time, time is winding up;
> 'Struction's in the land
> God's gonna move His hand.
> Time is winding up.

Placed on the matchless wings of a haunting melody, and to my knowledge never recorded or published, this verse reveals an awareness of the fact that things are so bad that "something's got to give." In spite of what the theologically oriented would call a crude eschatology, the verse is aware of the passing of an era. It is the funeral dirge for a dying age. This verse stands shoulder to shoulder with those words which came from a "seer" on the rocky, volcanic hills of an ancient island called Patmos. The seer there wrote in Revelation 21:1, "Then I saw a new heaven and a new earth; for the first heaven and the first earth had passed away. . . ." Here, again, the words have in mind persons whose existence was made virtually unbearable because of bloody persecution and ungodly dehumanization. The verse stands with the late Roi Ottley's book of a generation ago *New World A-Coming* in which he says the new world needed is actually the old world washed clean. The word is that there is a change in sight.

Much of the shape of the new world that is coming into being will be determined by you who still take religion seriously. You can make it a world of light and promise and wonder and excitement and freedom, or you can make of it a world as bad as or worse than that which we now know. I call upon you to give moral content and quality to the struggle for light and truth.

> Time, time, time is winding up!
> 'Struction's in the land
> God's gonna move His hand.
> Time is winding up.

"Then I saw a new heaven and a new earth; for the first heaven and the first earth had passed away. . . ."

I

"THE TIME IS WINDING UP!"

For one thing, this little verse reminds us of the fact that time is a factor in our situation. Let me hasten to add that I do not have the temerity to suggest that time will solve our problems. (Time does *not* always heal all wounds, *nor* does it always wound all heels.) I mean that time is involved in the sense that it is time that adds the dimension of urgency to the important. Sometimes the gaps which separate us, generationally, racially, economically, are the result, in some measure, of the kind of answer given to the question "When?" We are certainly familiar with the arguments of gradualism on the part of those categorized as conservatives and immediacy on the part of progressives, radicals, or what have you.

Men have pondered the matter of time. Is time a platform on which history stages the drama of life? Is it the road upon which the tramping feet of events travel? It has been suggested that Isaac Watts had the saints singing the strophes of Newtonian mechanics as they sang, and still sing, in a familiar hymn:

> Time, like an ever-rolling stream,
> Bears all its sons away;
> Then fly forgotten, as a dream
> Dies at the opening day.

In *Hyperion,* Longfellow raised the question and provided his answer: "What is time? The shadow on the dial, the striking of the clock, the running of the sand, day and night, summer and winter, months, years, centuries—these are but arbitrary and outward signs, the measure of Time, not Time itself. Time is the Life of the soul." So what has happened to the time that has gone by speaks of the deepest that there is about us—the soul. The true question, then, is what has happened to the soul—the self or life. Some could speak in the mood of the dreary soliloquy of Macbeth:

> To-morrow, and to-morrow, and to-morrow,
> Creeps in this petty pace from day to day,
> To the last syllable of recorded time;
> And all our yesterdays have lighted fools
> The way to dusty death. Out, out, brief candle!
> Life's but a walking shadow; a poor player,
> That struts and frets his hour upon the stage,
> And then is heard no more: it is a tale
> Told by an idiot, full of sound and fury,
> Signifying nothing.

To recall some of the events with which recent time has been pregnant is to see some real meaning in the dreary commentary of Macbeth that life is like a "tale told by an idiot, full of sound and fury, signifying nothing." Here is a huge band of the nation's poor marching to the capital of the nation as a dramatic reminder of the fact that in a land of plenty there are so many without the bare necessities.

A bloody event of recent times was the brutal murder of our country's most distinguished apostle of peace, Martin Luther King, Jr. Perhaps more are guilty than the person who pulled the trigger and fired the fatal shot. The question comes: "Were you there?" Well, where were you? And, where *are* you?

Robert F. Kennedy, saying and promoting many of the right things for our society, was shot. Murdered. There were senseless murders in Orangeburg, South Carolina, and Jackson State College and Kent State University. You have heard articulate intellectual and spiritual dwarfs decry the symptoms while completely ignoring the real root problems. You know of the blood of God's people of many descriptions that saturates the rice paddies of Vietnam because blind men sit in seats of authority.

In less dramatic fashion others have died and are now dying. Where do you stand? Where are you?

These are some of the pock marks of the diseased old world. These are some of the events of recent time. They belong to the time that is winding up. Now the big question comes: "What will the new era be like?" That question, you see, is directed to you. The people who take religion seriously are not out of it yet. Eyes will continue to be fastened on you to see what you are going to do with the times. Will the world which *you* make bear the pock marks of the old? Will it be but a tragic duplication of the old, or will it be truly a bright, new world? If we are prophets of light and truth, we are working for a bright, new world:

> Time, time, time is winding up!
> 'Struction's in the land
> God's gonna move His hand.
> Time is winding up.

"Then I saw a new heaven and a new earth; for the first heaven and the first earth had passed away. . . ."

II

"'STRUCTION'S IN THE LAND"

We cannot avoid the realization of the truth of the line of the spiritual which says "'Struction's in the land." What are we to do about this destruction? I offer two suggestions:

First, seek to discover the creative function of the conflict which now exists among us. Unfortunately, there are those who prefer an unreal peace to an honest confrontation with truth. Theologians and sociologists alike contend that conflict is evil and must be viewed in this manner. They are content with the mythical "peace and stability" model of society.

There are others, however, who recognize that the existence of conflict is not in and of itself bad. This is not to encourage the pointless, unprovoked creation of conflict. Rather, it is the realization of the fact, as J. Lawrence Burkholder puts it in the Harvard Divinity *Bulletin,* "A society without conflict is an historical impossibility."

Sociologists and philosophers who accept the conflict model of society point to the fact that much of tremendous value accrues to society because of the creative function of conflict. Conflict helps in the formation of group ego and group consciousness. It seems a rather strange paradox that discord and controversy sometimes serve to hold groups together and to bring out their best. If anybody knows this, most assuredly black people do.

Much of our best speaking, our best music, and our best strategy came out of situations of conflict. With our backs against the walls, we came forth with the spirituals and the blues. The genius of a Nat Turner or a Sojourner Truth arose out of situations of great conflict. The greatness of Martin Luther King and James Baldwin and Malcolm X came to the fore because they were caught up in situations of conflict. And an array of others found the same.

So if you are going to be more than a mere vegetable in this society, you will be involved in conflict—for there is "'struction in the land." Further, there is the example of Jesus Christ who stated that it would confuse some when they discovered that his coming would be divisive, that conflict would result. "I come not to bring peace, but a sword," he once said. Those seem to be pretty rough words coming from the lips of the "Prince of Peace!" He is here merely pointing out that when righteousness is confronted with unrighteousness, conflict results. I say to you that in the pursuit of the course of righteousness and justice and freedom and equality you will become involved in conflict, but so let it be. You are thus in high company. Search for and find its creative aspects.

A second suggestion is that we recognize the interim nature of much that is now going on. In moving from one era to another —one world to another—we find ourselves caught in that weird "between the ages" period. We are, in a sense, caught between two worlds. This means that we are under the influence of both.

Many of the values of our day are like the beginning of the baseball season when only a few games have been played and the team that is on top deserves to be there, but as the season progresses, it will fall into its rightful place.

Distinguishing the interim values from the ultimate ones is quite a task. This is the challenge set before us.

> Time, time, time is winding up!
> 'Struction's in the land
> God's gonna move His hand.
> Time is winding up.

III

"GOD'S GONNA MOVE HIS HAND"

What a reassuring word this is! It reminds us of the fact that the mighty hand of God moves across the pages of human history. It says to us that man is no hapless orphan deserted on the doorsteps of destiny, but that there is a Divine Creator and moral Governor of the universe. It says to us that although man violates the intent of God's design with his disorder, the last word is not left with man, but with God.

To be sure, there are those who look upon you with pity if they feel that you are taking seriously all of this God stuff. This is the time when men have proclaimed the untimely demise of God and have insisted upon the obsolescence of the Christian church. Yet, there are those who have not given up on the idea because of certain irrefutable experiences upon which they stand.

I have a word to say about the church. Now I know what the negative side is. As the late Kyle Haselden has said, "The church is often simply our culture having a polite conversation with itself." But let us not take lightly the church in the black community. The church among black people has been the social cosmos; it has provided an emotional outlet, a veritable safety valve, for people caught up in the whirling storms of life and has taught them to sing "We'll stand the storm, it won't be long; we'll

TIME IS WINDING UP! • 69

anchor bye and bye." She has been a source of inspiration and entertainment, of movements and plans which have moved the entire nation, and of leaders of courage and genius.

The black church has not gotten hopelessly hung up on moralisms as so many other expressions of the church in this country.

The black church is not hung up on tight structures and methodologies; thus there is flexibility and room for adaptation.

The black church has an historic interest in the social problems of our people. Even in the "otherworldly" emphasis of the past, the church among black people has gotten in some stinging attacks on social evil. It was an attack upon the hypocrisy of the religion of their slaveholders when they sang "everybody talking 'bout heaven ain't goin' there." And for a people who had been taught that they must be given inferior status and restricted territory not only on earth but even in "the celestial city," it was quite perceptive and audacious for them to sing "I'm going to walk *all over God's* heaven." Now, the otherworldly emphasis is greatly diminished as it gives way to an increased social aggression. To a significant degree, the church is the center of social action in many communities.

I submit that more crucial decisions have been made for our social betterment within the walls of the black church than any place else in our society—including the Supreme Court. I submit, further, that even in this day, there is no agency among us which can serve a greater purpose in helping us deal with our current social dilemmas than the black church. She has a message for the whole of Christendom; will we listen?

The church can help us keep the faith and stay tuned as we move from one age to another. I was once marginally listening to the television when I heard an announcer state that the next program was the "soap opera" called "Another World." But the words used are suggestive for us here. He said, "Stay tuned for 'Another World.'" This is what we must be willing to do ourselves and cause others to do. Don't tune the world out!

> Time, time, time is winding up!
> 'Struction's in the land
> God's gonna move His hand.
> Time is winding up.

"Then I saw a new heaven and a new earth; for the first heaven and the first earth had passed away. . . ."

Herman H. Watts is minister of Friendship Baptist Church in New York City. A graduate of Virginia Union University and Virginia Union University School of Religion, he has taken advanced work at Boston University and Union Theological Seminary. Before moving to New York, he was pastor in Camden, New Jersey, and in Virginia. He organized the South Jersey O.I.C. and now heads the Harlem branch of O.I.C. He also serves on the board of the YMCA in Harlem, as he had done in Camden. He has been active in the struggle to open employment opportunities to blacks and to improve housing in the community.

WHAT IS YOUR NAME?
Herman H. Watts

Every person comes into this world seeking his name. This is the centrality of life. By one's name is not meant the name upon a birth certificate, nor the name by which one's parents call him. Rather, what is the name by which God knows you? What is your essential alignment with the universe? What is your real purpose for living? How can you justify occupying space on this planet? How can we justify the air we breathe and the food we eat? What is your "raison d'être"?

Even people whose God is as mechanical as merely a "first cause" must recognize that there is order and planning in the universe; there is no lost motion, no wasted material, no useless personality. There is precision and exactness in the order of things. He who made us and made the cosmos had utter respect for law, order, and material; thus every person has a name, a place, and a responsibility for which no other can answer. No matter what one's definition of religion, it is his own personal name that gives relevance to it. Suppose one says his religion is the conservation of values, then his name is the role he takes in the conservation of values.

A person cannot live at his best and highest unless he has some primary name. One of the reasons for our schizophrenia and psychosis is the difficulty of feeling the thin whisper of reality calling us by our name. It is no easy matter. There are many voices calling us. One voice tells us to look out for ourselves and don't worry about others. Against that voice, another voice calls and says, "Your name is bigger than yourself; live for others!" We are torn, fragmented, distorted, and confused. The wailing cry of conflicting voices will not be quieted! In the commotion I lose my name, I forget my true identity.

Can we enlarge the canvas to the size of the planet? A nation struggles against other nations and against itself. What is the name of our beloved nation? What is its role? This amalgam of people, of history, of resources—what is the meaning of it all? Our nation is torn within and feels threatened without. Where do we stand? What of this nation whose name in yesteryear was life, liberty, and the pursuit of happiness?

Our demonstrations, murder, political chicanery, hatred, and strife are but symptoms of a psychopath who has forgotten his name. The pain, the guilt, and frustration break us.

Well, one day Jesus met a man like that (Luke 8:26-39). The man's utter frustration drove him from the company of loved ones. His drained strength canceled any attempt at gainful employment. He was a stranger to himself and a dead person to his family. His living death expressed itself in his wild eyes. His eyes had lost focus; his movements were unmeaningful; his speech produced irrational sounds. Such a man could exist only among the dead in the graveyard. The loneliness and estrangement of his soul could be symbolized by the unhearing, uncaring, and cold tombstones. The fierceness of his troubled soul was marked by the chains that held him. A man in a madhouse is exactly what he was. So unhappy, so miserable was his torment that he broke every chain. He pulled up tombstones; his strength shorn of rationality was almost limitless. Jesus approached the madman and the first question was, "What is your name?" At once his problem had been singled out. The answer was not yet, but the problem had been identified. "I don't know my name," was his pathetic cry. I have so many names. Sometimes I am a Pharisee, sometimes a tax collector, and at other times a revolutionary; I am not sure. I don't know whether life is an opportunity to grasp or to give. I don't know what I want to be or do. Sometimes I feel momentarily satisfied in making money and my big decisions revolve around money, and yet there are other times when life seems too big and too beautiful to be encrusted with money. Life's adventure with eternity is too long to be chained with transient and material things. "My name is Legion; I have so many names." Sometimes my name is pleasure and I bathe my flesh in its silky comfort; yet there keeps coming back to me a whisper telling me that pleasure is not my destined way. What a paradox! When I focus on pleasure, my heart is unhappy.

When I would stay in my little corner, there comes a beckoning finger calling me by a bigger name. I am so torn that my soul is threadbare! I have so many names!

This colorful first-century story paints in some detail the malady of our world. It diagnoses the strenuous tearing in our soul. Modern psychology can give no further authenticity to the turmoil in our souls. We need a central theme around which to bend our lives. We need a golden chalice that can hold our garnered thoughts. A sword does not pierce well with many points; it needs a single stabbing point. We are familiar with what is commonly called genius: a person so locked in on one area of thought that he is consumed by it. One thought, one loyalty, one purpose is his. Indeed, he no longer holds an interest, but an interest seizes him and holds and claims him. That is the meaning of the Master's pronouncement: "He that loseth his life for my sake shall find it" (Matthew 10:39, KJV).

Even a nation can have such a singleness that its impact may never be lost. Go yonder, lift the vale of years from sleeping Rome, and examine her contribution in jurisprudence. Lift the fragile lace of ancient Greece and see the flower of philosophy. If you please, watch the men who march through and speak in the Old Testament and you will witness the mighty sword of Judaism. In the history of one tribe there was brought together for the first time the idea of God and holiness. There is no power that can stop a man or a nation single-eyed on a great purpose. Can a nation be truly committed to helping the fallen when it spends as much of its thought and concern on those who already have attained? Can a nation be fully committed to peace when so much of its energies go for making war? Goethe said he was drawn by two horses—one black and one white—each pulling in different ways.

Another sage has said that there was a devil and an angel at war within him. Listen to the tortured cry of Paul: "The good that I would I do not: but the evil which I would not, that I do. . . . O wretched man that I am! who shall deliver me . . . ?" (Romans 7:19, 24, KJV).

The nature of a person's name depends upon his endowments. A person, to answer to his true name, must recognize that his name is different from all others that ever walked the face of the planet. Nature's God is so resourceful that he breaks the mold and destroys it forever. We waste our energies and torture our years trying to be like someone else. Each person has a name that no other can bear. There is a beauty, a strength, and a glory that each person has of his own. The whole universe is thrown out of kilter when you shrink from your magnanimous responsibility. There is a huge slot you must fill. When you have drunk from the social stream of the human family, you can see from a vantage point others cannot climb. The full sweep of recorded history has passed before your eyes in panoramic procession. You have seen many of the mistakes and the hard won insights of the human family. Now from the vantage position you must take your place. Better still, let your place take you. If a person is to be freed from his frustrations and insecurities, he must surrender to something larger than himself. He must attempt to see life from the angle of eternity. Our lives must deal with the only thing on the planet that is eternal, and that is human personality.

A larger perspective helps one see his place better. Three workmen were doing the same work at a construction site. One man was asked what he was doing and he replied that he was breaking up stones. The second replied that he was earning $3 an hour. But the third man—though doing the same work—replied that he was making a cathedral fit for the kingdom of God. The third man was able to relate his name to God; he had an affinity with eternity which the others lacked. Psychologists tell us that most people use only 10 percent of their potential. Imagine what this world would be like if everyone lived up to 25 percent of his endowments. The name by which God calls us is a big name! It is not necessarily limited by race and contemporary considerations. The men and women who have really answered to their names have changed the streams of history.

One of the things that shatters modern man is the feeling that he does not count. One reason some people don't vote is that they feel that one vote is unimportant. Some would never walk in a demonstration because they feel that one more person makes no difference! There is impersonalization everywhere. Our bank knows us by a number. The employment office gives us a six-digit number. Our national government knows us by our Social Security number. The feeling of being lost oppresses us. We cannot have even the joy of making an article in a factory. Rather, we make only a small part at a machine. How lost we are! But Jesus says we are not numbers. We are not numbers in a huge file. We are citizens of eternity whose influence will cause a shock wave for all eternity. John Bunyan in Bedford's jail did not feel himself an isolated prisoner. Rather from that very point, he stood so tall his stature touched the sky; his *Pilgrim's Progress* was too powerful to be shut into Bedford's jail; it spilled over until from that very point an oasis flowed throughout the breadth of the human race.

Oh, how we struggle to break the fetters of our confinement! Sometimes our names seem so limited as to be inconsequential. We are shut in by the iron fetters of race, poverty, and lack of opportunities. Yet Jesus says that every soul is destined for the skies. We are shut in on every turn. On the left side is the date of birth. How can we influence life before birth? On the right side we are shut in by death. How can we influence life after death? Beneath us is only the coldness of the grave. Above us— we can jump only a few feet. And even if we can leap to the closer planets, our reach and influence is still much too limited. Oh, how we strain against the walls of this clay hut in which we live! And even while we live, we pressure our lives against the limitations of sickness and demented talents and a thousand barriers. Somewhere between the promise of birth and the dim certainty of death we stumble in our frustrations. Seldom do we realize the magnitude of our names. Among those who would not accept life's cruel limitations was a man who said:

> Stone walls do not a prison make
> Nor iron bars a cage.
> If I have freedom in my love,
> And in my soul am free
> Angels alone that soar above
> Enjoy such liberty.

One can recount with glad eagerness the known souls who have not accepted life's limitations but have risen to the true measure of their names.

The trouble is that we hear so many names, we don't recognize the full throbbed name when it comes. We are like blind men sitting beside the roadside begging. We keep asking for crumbs when there are whole loaves to be had. We accept small petty names, when our birthright is within our reach. Look at that boy who settles for a meager job when with a little effort he could rise to his full potential. Look at that girl who refuses a new opportunity for training; she accepts a diminished role when her talents and opportunities keep calling her by a larger name. We waste our years on "making a living" instead of living. We spend our years playing it safe. Life is not intended to be safe. A safe life has too small a name for a creature of eternity. Life at its noblest and highest has a hazard about it; it ponders tomorrow but does not know it; it sounds the depth of the ocean, but knows not the hazard of the bottom. Life at its best takes a chance on righteousness no matter the hazard, no matter the cost. Life, when answering to its true name, lifts on wings, feeling no visible hands supporting it.

A college boy wrote home to his father asking money. The father, whose resources were limited, wrote back that high living was worth low living. He was saying that a boy to live up to high ideals of promise and sacrifice must be willing to let his economic standard fall.

What is your name? Well, to answer to our best and truest name often costs a great deal. Look at that first-century tentmaker turned missionary. Answering to his true name cost him the joys of family, the security of home, the satisfaction of regular income. More than that, it meant he had to know the confines of Nero's prison; he had to know beatings and denial by friends, and he had to come to his end with only his aged manuscripts to keep him company. If this is the cost in answering to our true names, there are rewards. Paul had that inner satisfaction that no outside turmoil could dim. Hear that rhetorical cry: "Who shall separate us from the love of Christ? Shall tribulation, or distress, or persecution, or famine, or nakedness, or peril, or sword?" Then comes that glad affirmation of faith, "Nay, in all these things we are more than conquerors through him that loved us" (Romans 8:35, 37, KJV). Here was a man flinging his life toward the height and depth of his true name.

When one looks back across the years and oceans and remembers the only saint that ever walked the planet, he sees a man—no less than you and me—seeking his true identity. Can one not read the record and see a child breaking the tender ties of home at twelve and beginning to move toward his true name? Though fate has hidden from us the years from twelve to thirty, we can assume from the fragments we do have that a great war raged in his soul. Many names claimed his life. Are not the symbolic and colorful temptations in the wilderness but a record of the inner conflict screaming in his soul? The claims of popularity, wealth, and earthly power forced themselves upon him in deadly procession. Yet in the end he submitted to the highest role. And he heard a voice from eternities saying, "This is my beloved Son, in whom I am well pleased" (Matthew 3:17, KJV).

One liberal scholar has said that it was not so much that God chose Jesus as Jesus chose God. Like Israel—not so much God chose Israel, but Israel chose God. It cost Jesus all to make a total commitment. He had to give up his close friends in the hamlets of Galilee. He had to give up Mother, finally to commit her to John. He moved steadily toward his true name. He flinched once at the cost when he said, "O my Father, if it be possible, let this cup pass from me . . ." (Matthew 26:39, KJV). Yet, once he set his eyes like flint to go, there was no turning back. The cost was of cosmic proportions—earth reeling and darkness at noonday, and finally his body twisting into a cruel question mark and asking "WHY?" The cost was stupendous! But the rewards and results changed this planet forever. Life could never be the same. The dead could get up. Religion could never be the

WHAT IS YOUR NAME? • 77

same—the veil in the temple was torn in twain—no intermediary to God now. Pain and blood could never be the same—they became the instruments of God's washing now. The cosmos could never be the same—it surrendered its equilibrium to moral impact. Death could never be the same; it is now the vehicle of lives too big for flesh and blood. Even the cross—the ancient symbol of dishonor, pain, and death—now became the cosmic instrument of salvation.

What is your name? Is it a small darkened shadow? Is it just to make a living? Is it merely an opportunity to get the best seats as we ride this planet to its docking station? Is it merely an opportunity to gather life's perishables? If these crumbs are your goals and commitments, then your name is Swine. But if you see the beckoning of the stars, if you hear the whisper of eternity, if you are willing to lose your life to find it, if you are willing to reflect the promise of the sunrise and the glory of the sunset—then get up; you are a fit candidate for eternity. Your name is written in the skies; your personality is part of the warp and woof of the very universe.

Stand tall; make a difference. No obstacle of race, religion, poverty, or geography can stop a life committed to God. At the core of reality there is life and love and dependability. We call that reality God. He knows, loves, and claims a life raised to the stature of its true name.

*Hosea L. Williams is the National Program Director of the South-
ern Christian Leadership Conference. A native of Georgia, he
attended Morris Brown College in Atlanta, Georgia, and Atlanta
University. He has been one of the leading figures in the civil
rights movement, leading many of the demonstrations and serving
as national mobilizer of the 1968 Poor People's Campaign. He
was chief organizer and director of the black political campaign
in Greene County, Alabama, which led to black control of political
affairs in the county. He is a national board member of the National Black Coalition, the National Committee of Black Churchmen, and the New Party, in addition to involvement in many
other organizations. He has received numerous awards for his
work in the field of civil rights.*

THE RELEVANCY OF THE BLACK CHURCH
TO THE NOW GENERATION
Hosea L. Williams

I want you to know I am honored to have the opportunity to
preach to you this morning, for we who are involved full-time
in the movement, we who have accepted a black theology, we
livers of a black religion, we who are defined by the white press
as "irresponsible negroes," we who are not popular among the
Negro middle class—the rich, the well-educated, the elite—we
who refuse to be co-opted or brainwashed by the power structure,
the Pharaohs of today, we who have held up the bloodstained
banner, we troublemakers—thank God, the devils call us the
agitators—are not often invited by churches or pastors to preach

or to speak to their youth. They say that we'll teach them some bad habits, we'll start some trouble.

I say to you young people here this morning, I am convinced what you are now involved in is the only way to redeem the soul of this sick nation. It is the only way to make the dream of our great, beloved, fallen leader, Dr. Martin Luther King, Jr., come true. It is the only way, as our Father has taught us, "Our Father, who art in heaven, hallowed be thy name, thy kingdom come, thy will be done, on earth as it is in heaven." This is the only way to bring God's kingdom upon this earth.

The sin, the evil that is destroying this nation and that will eventually destroy the world, will never be eliminated by the legislatures, governmental bodies, volunteer social agencies, fraternal organizations, or the church.

I'm talking about black religion as the only answer to Satan's destruction of mankind.

So I would like to speak to you this morning from the subject: *The Relevancy of the Black Church to the Now Generation.*

Let's just simplify our subject by calling it *black religion.* Because in my theology the only religion that is relevant is black religion, and black religion is only relevant to the now generation.

When I speak of the now generation, I am not speaking of the chronological age; I'm not speaking of the age of an individual according to the number of years he or she has lived, for an individual is only as old as he thinks.

There are some old people, some "Uncle Toms," some "Aunt Tomasinas," some handkerchief-head Nellies, some deceivers of Jesus Christ between the ages of ten and twenty; for there are some of you who have already accepted white religion, and you can't accept white religion unless you have rejected the relevant religion which is the black religion.

To me, Lillian Smith, the author of *The Killers of the Dream,* adequately defined white religion when she talked of how religious some of us are on Sunday, how crowded the churches are on Sunday, and how we pray and how we sing. Some of us even shout. She talked about how graciously we worshiped God on Sunday, but from Monday through Saturday we only think of ourselves. We only think about how much money we can make. We only think of what kind of house our family can live in. We only think of what kind of school our children can go to.

In fact, we don't give a damn about our neighbors. To me, that is a white religion.

The nineteenth chapter, the sixteenth verse of Matthew talks of a white religion when a young, rich ruler came to Jesus and said, "Teacher, what good deeds must I do to have a relevant religion?"

And Jesus told him to keep the commandments.

The rich, young ruler said, "This I have done. What else do I lack?"

Jesus said to him, "If you want a relevant religion, go and sell what you possess, take the money and distribute it among the prostitutes, the pimps, the punks. Distribute it among the uneducated, the jobless, the welfare mothers.

"Distribute your money among the hungry of the blackbelt of the southland. Go and distribute it among the dope addicts of the black ghettos and you will have treasures in heaven and come follow me."

"When the young man heard this he went away sorrowful; for he had great possessions" (Matthew 19:22, RSV). He preferred an irrelevant religion, a white religion.

The Scripture goes on to tell us that Jesus then said to his disciples, "Truly, I say to you, it is harder for a rich man to enter the kingdom of heaven"—it is harder for a rich man to accept a black religion, a relevant religion—"than it is for a camel to go through the eye of a needle." (See Matthew 19:23-24.)

Now let's remember, God never indicted wealth, but he has indicted the use of wealth and has condemned those who have preferred wealth to a black religion.

In the sixteenth chapter, the nineteenth verse of Luke, Jesus spoke to the Pharisees:

There was a certain rich man who dressed fabulously and ate sumptuously every day. At the gate of his expensive, ranch-style, suburban home was a sick man by the name of Lazarus.

Lazarus was from the ghetto. He was unemployed. He was raggedy and dirty. Lazarus was hungry, begging for food. He only wanted the crumbs, the leftovers from the rich man's table.

But instead of the rich man helping this poor man by feeding him the scraps from his table, he turned him away and said that he was not a responsible Negro; said that he was not liked by the power structure; said that he was not dressed well. He was not clean. Therefore, he would not even give him the scraps, the left-overs from his table.

Lazarus fell down along the wayside of life. He became a school dropout. He was unemployed, couldn't find a job. He was forced to rob and steal for a living.

Our Lazarus of today comes sometimes in the form of a prostitute who has to sell her body to feed her young'uns. Today's Lazarus sometimes comes in the form of a drug addict, who out of frustration and desperation has resorted to heroin.

Anyway, the Bible teaches us that Lazarus fell down and was unable to receive even the crumbs from the rich man's table—the man who had accepted a white man's religion, the man who belonged to a church that was confined to four walls, a church that got its respectability from man and not from God, a church where people live a white religion, a church that has its arms open, beckoning to the rich, the educated, a church beckoning to the so-called responsible Negroes.

The rich man did not feed Lazarus but instead allowed his dogs to lick the sores of Lazarus's body.

Lazarus—this poor man—died and went on to heaven. Our Bible teaches us that the rich man also died, but he went to Hell.

He didn't go to Hell because of his wealth. He went to Hell because of his misuse of wealth. That is what I call a *white religion.*

But, while this rich man, a millionaire, was sent to Hell for the misuse of wealth, for accepting a white religion, for overlooking Lazarus; there was a *billionaire* in heaven by the name of Abraham.

In testing Jesus, a lawyer asked him one day, "Teacher, what shall I do to inherit eternal life?" (Luke 10:25, RSV).

Jesus asked him, "You are learned, what is the law?"

And the lawyer said, "Love your God with all your heart, all your soul, all your strength, and all your mind. In other words, love God with everything you have, and love your neighbor as yourself."

And Jesus said, "You are right."

And the lawyer asked, "But who is my neighbor?"

Jesus said, "There was a black man one day traveling from Selma, Alabama, to Birmingham, Alabama. He had to go through some terrible territory. That man was beaten and robbed and left to die, unconscious, beside the road, by some white racists.

"Or, he might have been beaten and robbed and left to die by some Uncle Toms or some Aunt Tomasinas.

"Or, he just might have been beaten and robbed and left to die by some of those so-called Christians who go to church and serve God on Sunday, but they become selfish and serve the devil all the week.

"Anyway, there came along a preacher, a minister. Some call this man a rabbi, a priest, riding along in his nice automobile. This preacher of a white religion, this preacher who didn't like to be seen with poor people from the ghetto, saw this man lying along highway 80 and noticed the man had been beaten and robbed, obviously left to die.

"Knowing he may get himself dirty if he stopped and picked up this man, knowing that he might be seen helping a drug addict or a robber, knowing that this man obviously was broke and not able to pay large church dues, this preacher passed him by.

"Our Scripture teaches us then there came one of his own kind—a soul brother—according to the *Atlanta Constitution,* a so-called responsible Negro who was educated, who was respected because of his wealth. He might have made his money through cheating uneducated people; he might have made his money through financing the dope racket, or running a house of prostitution where young women are forced to sell their bodies to make a living.

"However, this man was highly respected because he had a lot of money. He had accepted a white religion and also made the greenback dollar bill one of his gods.

"But anyway, this responsible Negro stopped his Cadillac and looked upon this black man who had been beaten and robbed and left to die, but he did not want to get his silk suit soiled or his new Cadillac bloody. For he saw how badly this man had been beaten and surely if he put him into his car and carried him to the hospital, his Cadillac would get bloody.

"Therefore, he also passed him by.

"Then, there came one, the third man, who knew Jesus, a man who had gone to jail for the rights of his people, a man who had marched in the streets of America so that his people some day would be free, a man who was a member of a church that had no walls, a man who was part of that church that Jesus spoke about when he said, 'Upon this rock I will build my church, and the gates of Hell cannot prevail against it.' "

And I am sure, my friends, when Jesus spoke of the gates of Hell, he spoke of the gates of poverty, the gates of crime, the gates of drug addiction, the gates of prostitution, the gates of welfare, the gates of unemployment.

Jesus was speaking of all the hells that today's church must conquer—not the legislatures, not the volunteer agencies—but the church, this church which is carrying on a black religion; in fact, this man we are talking about who was also traveling from Selma to Montgomery and saw this black brother who had been beaten, who had been robbed, who had been left to die.

Because this man served God not only on Sunday, but every day in the week, because this man knew he could not love God whom he had never seen unless he loved his brother who had been beaten and robbed and left to die, he stopped his car and he got out. He went over to him and he first tried to comfort him and give him confidence and assurance in himself by telling him:

"You might have been beaten and robbed, but I want to help you because you are somebody. You may be black, but you are somebody." Then he got out his pocket handkerchief and began to wipe the blood and the dirt from the man's aching wounds.

He then got him up, put him in his car, and carried him on to the hospital.

When he got to the hospital, he carried him to the emergency room and the first thing the people at the hospital wanted to know was, "Did he have insurance?"

And this good Samaritan, this man with the black religion said, "I don't know, but I have some money."

Then he was told by the hospital officials, "You will have to have a $50 deposit."

The man said, "Well, I have $60 on me. Here's $50 deposit. Admit him and give him medical care."

While the doctors were stitching and binding the wounds of the beaten man, someone came and told this good Samaritan, "He's going to be all right, but he will have to be hospitalized."

He then pulled out his American Express courtesy card and said, "I must be going on my way, but I would like to sign a blank, and you stamp my credit card and charge whatever the balance is for curing this man."

Then Jesus said to the lawyer, "Which of these three men do you think proved to be a neighbor? Which of these three men had a black religion?"

I say to you young people today, don't waste a good life. As our Bible teaches us, *what is it for a man to gain the world and lose his soul?*

Be a Christian. Being a Christian means following in the footsteps of Jesus; it means living a worthy life.

Remember, Jesus was thrown into jail cells for standing up to the power structure. Jesus was not popular among the scribes and the priests during his day. He had to bear a cross up Calvary's mountain. He died between two thieves.

Being a Christian, sometimes the pain will seem unbearable. In fact, they beat Jesus, nailed spikes through his hands, and split open his side. And at one point things got so terrible that Jesus looked up to heaven and said, *"Father, why hast thou forsaken me?"*

I define Christianity as a black religion because it is a religion of labor, a religion of giving. It is a religion of finding the greatest pleasure in life by helping those unable to help themselves.

Martin Luther King, Jr., had a black religion. He always dwelled among the lowly ones although he was one of the most influential, best educated men in the world. Loved by billions, he died while fighting for the rights of garbage men.

If Jesus lived today, someone would say, "There goes that old fool."

And you would say, "What old fool?"

"That old fool Jesus."

And you would say, "Why do you call him a fool? They say he's a good carpenter, and he built himself a nice home across town."

"But his neighbor lost his job and was evicted into the streets, and they tell me that old fool gave the neighbor his house."

If Jesus lived today, they would call him an old fool.

I say to you young people today, do not accept a white religion, do not accept a church that is confined within four walls. I say to you, do not run away from the church because the church has become irrelevant to your lives, for there is no answer in man.

So instead of running away from the church, that is, that church that has no walls, run to the church. Seize it and make it what Jesus intended for it to be when he said to Peter, *"Upon this rock I will build my church, and the gates of Hell cannot prevail against it."*

I remember just about a year or two ago, I started thinking about this. I went down to Birmingham, Alabama, to speak on Easter night. I parked the car and I started up to the church. There was a lady standing on the corner crying, shedding tears. I said, "Madam, what's the matter?"

She said, "Mister, don't bother me. Just go ahead, don't bother me."

I said, "Please tell me what's the matter."

And finally she told me. She said, "You see those people down there going in that church-house, with all those little girls with their shiny pocketbooks and with their new dresses and with their new bonnets? They are going in that church. This is Easter, Mister." She had three little girls who were dirty and raggedy. She said, "I'm on welfare. I'm on welfare and I can't afford to buy my daughters any new clothing. Mister, sometimes I don't even have money to buy these girls soap to wash their bodies. Mister, you get tired of going around always dirty and stinking."

Do you think, if that sister could not go in that church, do you have any idea that God was in there? Do you have any idea that God will go where his children are kept out?

If you have a black religion, you will accept that part of the Scripture which teaches us, "Go out into the world and preach my gospel."

Wherever we roam, that is God's church. We may be in the streets of Vine City, we may be in the streets of Sandersville, Georgia, we may be in the streets of Harlem, New York; but wherever we preach, that is God's church. A church without four walls.

Whenever you find a church confined by four walls, it is man's church. But I'm talking about a church where if the police beat our brothers on a Saturday night and the city council does not correct the injustice, the church will mess up the city on Monday. Whenever these big businesses deny our sisters and brothers a decent job to make an honest living, it is the church's duty to picket, to boycott, to march, or to do whatever it takes to force the Pharaohs to let our people go.

The acceptance and living of a black religion, thereby building a church with no walls that the gates of Hell cannot prevail against, is the only way to save man from self-destruction, is the only way to conquer the evils and the sins that are destroying our young people who will control the world of tomorrow.

I'm talking about selfishness. I'm talking about a life of profit motives, the subjugating of human values to material values, the making of a dollar bill our god.

I'm talking about conquering drug addiction, hunger, prostitution, robbery, rape, and murder.

I'm talking about black religion!!!!

Dr. Gayraud S. Wilmore is the Martin Luther King Professor of Social Ethics at the Boston University School of Theology. He was born in Philadelphia, Pennsylvania, and earned the A.B. and B.D. degrees from Lincoln University in Pennsylvania. He received the S.T.M. degree from Temple University School of Religion and took additional graduate work at Temple and also Drew University. He has served as a pastor, a teacher, and most recently as the Executive Director of the Council on Church and Race of the United Presbyterian Church in the U.S.A. He was Director of the American Forum for International Studies in the summer of 1971 at the University of Ghana in Accra and the Joseph Cook Lecturer in S.E. Asia in 1972. He is the author of many magazine and journal articles. A life member of the N.A.A.C.P., he is also a member of the Board of the National Committee of Black Churchmen as well as many other boards and committees.

BLACK THEOLOGY
Gayraud S. Wilmore

"The Spirit of the Lord is upon me,
   because he has anointed me to preach good news to the poor.
He has sent me to proclaim release to the captives
   and recovering of sight to the blind,
   to set at liberty those who are oppressed."

Luke 4:18 (RSV)

An editorial in the *Christian Century* reproached the United Methodist Church for ignoring the work of the brilliant young black theologian James H. Cone, now teaching at Union Theological Seminary in New York City. Cone, said the *Christian Cen-*

tury editor, is better known and more appreciated by European theologians than he is in his own country. The editor raised the question of whether black theologians, like many black singers, artists, poets, and conductors, will have to go to Europe and get some attention before they are taken seriously by their own countrymen.[1]

But an even more shocking indictment can be made. Not only is Cone not known among white churchmen in this country— very little is known about him among black Christians. Indeed, even among black college people taking courses in Black Studies, the new black theology and new work being done by black theologians like James Cone are relatively unknown.

That is why I want to talk about black theology.

We are, it has been said, a religious people. Religion has had an enormous significance in the life and culture of our people. There have been, however, two parallel streams of religious influence in our history—not equally favorable to our development as a free people.

One has been the almost wholesale adaptation of the world-denying, pietistic, individualistic religion of the white man—the religion of white theology, a religion, sad to say, still operative in many black churches today. The other is the world-affirming, revolutionary religion related to our oppression and our longing for liberation, a religion often resisted but never completely blotted out of the life of the black church and one that is being resurrected today by some of our younger theologians under the rubric of black theology.

The text of Genesis 1:27 provides a suitable warrant for what we are calling "Black Theology."

> So God created man in his own image, in the image of God he created him.

Theology is man's thought about God in the light of what God is doing about man. If you are black and you were created in the image of God, then for you, in more than a superficial sense, God is black and your thoughts about him—your theology, in order to be authentic—must be black theology.

Black theology is thinking about God and the meaning of your

[1] Cornish Rogers, "James Cone and the Methodists," *Christian Century,* November 17, 1971, p. 1340.

life in relation to God, your Creator, out of the experience of being born black and living as a black man in this world.

Wherever we speak of a black theology, eyebrows rise in a white congregation, but almost as frequently among middle-class blacks. Why so? You have heard of a German theology, a French Catholic theology, a Jewish theology. What is so strange about a black theology? Every group of people, every race, thinks about God out of its own state of being, its own understanding of itself, out of its own condition of life. Look at the various racial pictorializations of God—the northern European, the medieval Italian, the Japanese, the Chinese, the American Indian.

Some black men have always thought about God out of the condition and experience of blackness. "God created man in his own image, in the image of God he created him." Black theology needs no other justification. What we have in black theology, as in American white theology, is a partial, provisional, but wholly satisfactory truth about God as a working hypothesis for black life as we understand it and believe that God wills for us to live it today.

I

The search for a meaningful and relevant way for black people to talk about God goes back to Africa. Black theologians are becoming increasingly interested in African religions because we now believe that God had manifested himself on that continent before the white missionary and slave trader arrived—and because we have never completely lost the rich religious and cultural heritage of our African past.

Our children need to know that black people did not come into existence on the auction blocks of Richmond, Charleston, and New Orleans. Nor did our religious consciousness begin with the preaching of Christianity. The missionaries tried their best to stamp out the survivals of African religions in early black Christianity, but they couldn't quite bring it off.

Today some black theologians are trying to recover some of the major themes and values of those traditional religions of Nigeria, Dahomey, Ghana, and the other places from which most of our ancestors came. From where else did we get the deep sense of the pervasive reality of the spirit world, the blotting out of the line between the sacred and the profane, the practical use of religion in all of daily life, the reverence of our culture heroes and their presence with us, the corporateness of social life, the source of evil in the consequences of an act rather than in the act itself, and the free utilization of rhythm, drum, singing, and dancing in the worship of God? Of course, these are all parts of our African heritage.

They lie in the dim reaches of our history, but they have, by no means, been expunged from our religious tradition. All of these aspects of African religions were found, in some form, in the religion of our slave forefathers and became combined with Christianity in the Caribbean, in South America, and in the United States. Black theology today wants to recover these values and to apply them to our situation today—particularly, the African emphasis on feeling, spontaneity, and freedom in religion and life, which had so much to do with the resistance of black religion to complete "whitenization."

Black theology today is not simply concerned with political liberation any more than slave religion was concerned simply or exclusively with emancipation. Black theology is concerned with freedom as existential deliverance or liberation from every force that restrains and inhibits the full, spontaneous release of the black body, mind, and soul from internal and external bondage— of whatever sort. African religions were deeply concerned about freedom, as were all so-called primitive religions. It is no accident that our fathers sang:

> "O Freedom, O Freedom over me. And before I'll
> be a slave, I'll be buried in my grave, and go home
> to my Lord, and be free."

That was the beginning of black theology. Black theology today is concerned about the meaning and the achievement of that freedom—the freedom to be *Muntu*—a man or a woman, in the most profound meaning of that profound Bantu word.

II

The second level of the search for a black theology takes us into the meaning of the religion of the slaves. Our forefathers were not able to keep their African religions. They received the Christian doctrine of salvation through the life, death, and resurrection of Jesus Christ. But they rejected it out of hand; they could not quite understand how anyone who really taught the message of love could insist upon holding them in one of the most brutal forms of slavery the world had ever known.

What they rejected was not so much the gospel, but the white interpretation of "goodness," "truth," "will of God," "being saved." While the white men taught them one thing, they secretly believed another and began, in the seventeenth and eighteenth centuries, to shape their own version of Christian faith.

The Rev. C. C. Jones, a famous white missionary to the slaves, tells the story of how once when he was preaching to slaves on the text from Ephesians 6: "Servants be obedient to your masters," half of the congregation got up and walked out. Those who remained told him there was no such text in the Bible and that he should not come back to preach to them again.

Moton tells of one Brother Armstead Barkley, the pastor of a Negro Baptist church, who was called upon to pray for the Confederate arms just after the battle of Gettysburg. "O Lord," he prayed, "point the bullets of the Confederate guns right at the hearts of the Yankees, make our men victorious on the battlefield, and send them home in health and strength to join their people in peace and prosperity." There were ten thousand people present. After the white folks left, the deacons gathered around and challenged Brother Barkley for taking white folks' side against the cause of his people. His reply in all seriousness was, "Don't worry, children. The Lord knows what I was talking about." And everybody was satisfied.

The Lord the slaves believed in and served knew what they were talking about and what they were interested in—and it was not the same thing that interested their masters. They may have used the same words, the same Bible, and the same creeds, but the Lord knew that they longed for a higher goodness, a truer truth, a more immediate salvation, and a more authentic church than Massa conceived of or would permit. The seminal black theology, in other words, secretly taught that God wanted black people to be free. "If the Son makes you free, you will be free indeed" (John 8:36, RSV). Our greatest fighters for freedom were religious leaders—Denmark Vesey, Nat Turner, David Walker, Henry Highland Garnet, and many others. The Negro spirituals reveal a tension between the traditional words of the faith and the longing of black people to be free. This longing led them to give a meaning to the words very different from that assumed by white Christians.

III

Thus far I have mentioned African religions and the secret religion of the slaves as two important sources of material for black theology. There is time to mention only one other—*the black experience in the ghetto today.* Black students and the black middle class still tend to forget that the essence of black religion is found not among the black elite, but in the ghetto. Langston Hughes has described the spirit of these people: "Their joy runs, bang! into ecstasy. Their religion soars to a shout. Work maybe a little today, rest a little tomorrow. Play awhile. Sing awhile. O, let's dance!"

It is from this reservoir of black culture—of which religion is an inseparable part—that black theology searches for the genius of what Joseph Washington calls "Negro Folk Religion," or "the religion of protest and relief." It was this folk religion that Marcus Garvey, Elijah Muhammad, and Malcolm X tapped into when they began to build their respective black nationalist movements. This same black folk religion came into its own in the southern civil rights movements under Dr. Martin Luther King, Jr. This same black folk religion is what underlies "Operation Breadbasket" and O.I.C. today. This same black folk religion, in a strange but unmistakable vesture, is coming to the surface today in the interpretations of black power by such people as Maulana Ron Karenga, Imamu Baraka, and Albert Cleage.

Black theology arises out of the questions that God is raising with his people wherever they are found. These questions relate to the everyday experience of black Christians—their hopes, dreams, sorrows, their awareness of the contradictions between the American dream and American reality. Black theology is saying that God speaks to us today in the accents of 125th Street and Lenox Avenue, of Soledad and Attica—that if God is anywhere, he is where black life is lived in its greatest exasperation, and it is the church's business to meet him, interpret him, and work with him there.

I began my ministry as an enthusiastic, idealistic young man, under the inspiration of Luke 4:18: "The Spirit of the Lord is upon me, because he has anointed me to preach good news to the poor. He has sent me to proclaim release to the captives and recovering of sight to the blind, to set at liberty those who are oppressed."

Since the time of my ordination, I have become increasingly disillusioned with the possibility of pursuing that kind of liberating ministry, a ministry to the "poor and oppressed" under the domination of main-line white Protestantism in the United States. What I looked for as central in Christian theology—the liberation of the oppressed—was only peripheral in white Christianity. Nor could it be otherwise than peripheral, secondary, a dangerously radical heresy in a church steeped in arrogant Calvinism, the evangelical pietism and the racism of American white Christianity.

I have not yet left the Presbyterian Church. Like many other black ministers, I am still agonizing over a vocation in an institution which has humiliated and oppressed my people for over 250 years.

But the rediscovery of the theme of resistance and liberation in black religion has reassured some of us that God is not dead! He is striving with black humanity to reveal himself as deliverer in the context of the black experience—and to reveal us to ourselves in our true identity as a people of God.

The young black militants talk of political liberation, and rightly. But there can be no true black political liberation without religious and cultural liberation. As Harold Cruse has observed:

> As long as the Negro's cultural identity is in question, or open to self-doubts, then there can be no positive identification with the real demands of his political and economic existence. Further than that, without a cultural identity that adequately defines *himself*, the Negro cannot even identify with the American nation as a whole. He is left in the limbo of social marginality, alienated and directionless on the landscape of America.[3]

But religious tradition is an inseparable element in black cultural identity. Cruse, perhaps without knowing it, is defining the distinctive role of black religion to bring to a marginal, alienated, and directionless people the spiritual wealth of the black religious tradition—wholeness, reunion, and a divine destiny.

[3] Harold Cruse, *The Crisis of the Negro Intellectual* (New York: William Morrow Co., 1967), pp. 12-13.

The task of black theology then is first to bring liberation to black people, but its greatness is even beyond that achievement. A revitalized, revolutionary black religion has an unsurpassable contribution to make to world Christianity today. I must agree with James Baldwin who has many times reminded us that it may be given to black Americans to yet save this racist nation. That well may be the task of black religion in the years to come.

The church of Christ needs the legacy of black theology for the quest for freedom, dignity, and self-determination. This is to say that the meaning of Luke 4:18, "To set at liberty those who are oppressed," is the shape of God's future for all mankind. And only black Christians who know themselves to have been created, in all their blackness, in the image of God and who know that he shares their suffering and misery for a purpose can be the agents through which that future breaks in upon us and upon all nations of men.

Once again, in the history of the black church, we are persuaded that, like his Son, those who were despised and rejected by men have been chosen by God to bring his kingdom of love, liberation, peace, and freedom to fruition. May God bless our efforts as black churchmen and black theologians to find what he wants us to do.

SUGGESTED TOOLS FOR THE PREACHER
Walter B. Hoard

The preacher and his sermon are inseparable, like the carpenter and his saw. For some, preaching comes easy, but other men must labor to sharpen the tongue, to fill the pitcher as well as to remain relevant for the time.

Since the preached word has always been central in the black experience, the preacher has used every tool to give new dimensions of authority and power to his sermons. Even during slavery when the spiritual destiny of the slave community depended upon the black preacher, and his only tool seemed to be a pouring out of his suffering soul, the preacher kept to the Bible as his source of God's knowledge.

Not much has changed in the black pulpit. The preacher still is expected to determine the spiritual direction of the black community. He is expected to give the multitude a veritable "window of hope." He still stands on the sabbath mount surrounded by a perplexed multitude waiting for him to make sense out of injustice, racism, ecology, poverty. It is the black preacher who must be spiritually proficient and profoundly prophetic to assure the yearning crowd, week after week and year after year, that all of God's children are able to transcend the vicissitudes of human life.

To preach effectively requires, therefore, a constant searching and seeking process for clarity of the word, better methods, and good examples. The black pulpiteer hence uses whatever aids God sends him.

Historically the black preacher has found it necessary to draw from the various wells of Christian faith. As a result, the following sources are some typical tools.

WORSHIP RESOURCES
PUBLISHED BY JUDSON PRESS

Contemporary Biblical Interpretation for Preaching, Ronald J. Allen. 1984. Use critical exegesis in a simplified manner to develop fresh biblical interpretations for sermons. 0-8170-1002-5

Cups of Light . . . and Other Illustrations, Clarence W. Cranford. 1988. Two-hundred illustrations for sermons and meditations. 8-8170-1142-0

Dedication Services for Every Occasion, Manfred Holck, Jr., compiler. 1984. Thirty-five services for just about any special celebration. 0-8170-1033-5

God's Transforming Spirit: Black Church Renewal, Preston R. Washington. 1988. Discusses important elements of church renewal—prayer discipline, dependence on the Holy Spirit for guidance, helping members grow in discipleship, and ministry to the community. 0-8170-1129-3

Interpreting God's Word in Black Preaching, Warren H. Stewart. 1984. Five-point study of the hermeneutical process for interpreting and communicating the Word so that it will be relevant to the congregation. 0-8170-1021-1

Listening on Sunday for Sharing on Monday, William D. Thompson. 1983. How the preacher and the listening congregation can become a dynamic partnership for spreading the message of God's healing power. 0-8170-1000-9

Outstanding Black Sermons, J. Alfred Smith, ed. 1976. 0-8170-0664-8

Outstanding Black Sermons, Volume 2, Walter B. Hoard, ed. 1979. 0-8170-0832-2

Outstanding Black Sermons, Volume 3, Milton Owens, Jr., ed. 1982. 0-8170-0973

Prayers for All Occasions: For Pastors and Lay Leaders, Roy Pearson. 1990. 0-8170-1127-7

Sermons from the Black Pulpit, Samuel D. Proctor and William D. Watley. 1984. Thirteen sermons that call for a renewed commitment to discipleship. 0-8170-1034-3

Sermons on Special Days—Preaching Through the Year in the Black Church, William D. Watley. 1987. 0-8170-1089-0

Telling the Story: Evangelism in Black Churches, James O. Stallings. 1988. Challenges black Christians to recapture the power of their rich evangelistic heritage. 0-8170-1124-2

Those Preachin' Women, Ella Pearson Mitchell, ed. 1985. Fourteen sermons by black women that call Christians to develop positive attitudes and to find their identities by oneness in God. 0-8170-1073-4

Those Preaching Women, Volume 2, Ella Pearson Mitchell, ed. 1988. More sermons by black women. 0-8170-1131-5

Vision of Hope: Sermons for Community Outreach, Benjamin Greene, Jr., ed. 1988. Action-oriented sermons that offer a fresh view of the church's mandate for ministry to hurting people. 0-8170-1150-1

Women: To Preach or Not to Preach? 21 Outstanding Black Preachers Say Yes! Ella Pearson Mitchell, ed. 1991. 0-8170-1169-2